Envisioning
an
Empowered Nation

Technology for Societal Transformation

Royalty accrued to the authors through the sale of this book will be contributed to the "VIKSIT BHARAT (DEVELOPED INDIA) FOUNDATION", a non-profit society set up at Hyderabad. This will give a thrust to the 'Foundation' to initiate a few rural development projects for the vision of a Developed India by 2020.

Envisioning
an
Empowered Nation

Technology for Societal Transformation

Prof. A P J Abdul Kalam
with
Dr. A Sivathanu Pillai

Tata McGraw-Hill Publishing Company Limited
NEW DELHI

McGraw-Hill Offices

New Delhi   New York   St Louis   San Francisco   Auckland   Bogotá
Caracas   Kuala Lumpur   Lisbon   London   Madrid   Mexico City
Milan   Montreal   San Juan   Santiago   Singapore   Sydney   Tokyo   Toronto

Tata McGraw-Hill

© 2004, Tata McGraw-Hill Publishing Company Limited

This edition can be exported from India only by the publishers,
Tata McGraw-Hill Publishing Company Limited

ISBN 0-07-053154-4

Published by Tata McGraw-Hill Publishing Company Limited,
7 West Patel Nagar, New Delhi 110 008, typeset at Script Makers
19, A1-B, DDA Market, Pashchim Vihar, New Delhi 110 063 and printed at
Gopson Papers Ltd, Noida, India

Cover: Kapil Gupta

DCLYCDDIRABBR

The McGraw-Hill Companies

*The interactions with students and youth
from all parts of the country and the series
of lectures given to the engineering students
of Anna University, and students of other
universities, colleges and schools, resulted
in evolving this book. Hence*
**the book is dedicated to the youth and the
student community of India.**

Prologue

During the last four years, I have visited almost all parts of India and interacted with people from all walks of life— students, youth, farmers, scientists, engineers, technicians, doctors, medical staff, educationists, industrialists, armed forces personnel, spiritual leaders, political leaders, administrators, economists, artists, sports persons, physically and mentally challenged and the rural populace. *What have I learnt from these interactions across the different cross-sections of the Indian population?*

School children and youth also interacted with me through my website. They gave many suggestions on making India a developed nation and their role in achieving this mission. I would like to highlight a few of the suggestions, among the many, which I received from children and youth.

One student from Meghalaya responded, *"I enjoy teaching as it can shape children to be good citizens of our country. So I want to become a teacher or a soldier to defend my country"*. Another girl from Pondicherry said, *"A garland can be made only with many flowers with a common thread. Therefore, I will make my countrymen love the nation and work for the unity of minds to* realise the garland—Developed India". Another boy from Goa said, *"I would become an electron and just like an electron in the orbit, I will work ceaselessly for my country".* A boy of Indian origin based at Atlanta, responded, *"When India becomes self-reliant and has the capability to put sanctions against any country, if needed, then I will sing the song of India, and I will work for it".* The young boy meant that India should become a developed country with economic prosperity, accompanied with national security and political will.

What noble thoughts from the young minds! These are only examples. The aspiration of young ignited minds to make the nation great is evident. It is important to recognise that India has a population of 700 million such young minds. This is a large force, which needs to be harnessed constructively towards a singular mission of making India a developed country. Like the young, every citizen of India I interacted with, would like to live in a happy, prosperous, peaceful and safe India.

I have seen the beauty of our country in the deserts, mountains, seashores, forests and in the fields. India has a rich civilisation, heritage, resource, talented workforce and above all there is potential due to the emergence of a knowledge society. Still 26% of our population is below the poverty line, and illiteracy and large scale unemployment persist. While it is imperative to address these problems, it is also necessary to increase the economic growth. This can be achieved by an effective management of resources and manpower—our core competencies.

> *We must get rid of the inferiority complex and defeat the defeatist spirit that plagues us. We must celebrate our successes and encourage the talented to work for missions which will bring glory to India.*

Our Prime Minister during his address on the eve of Independence Day 2002, declared that India will become a

Developed Nation by 2020. The tenth five-year plan also focuses on an economic growth of 8% and an employment potential of one hundred million.

In recent years, technology has come to play a dominant role in improving the quality of life. Technology is the engine capable of driving a nation towards growth and prosperity, and giving it the necessary competitive edge in the comity of nations. Technology, thus, has an important role to play in transforming India into a developed country.

In my earlier book, "*India 2020—A vision for the new millennium*", written in 1998 with Shri Y S Rajan, we discussed the Technology Vision 2020 by TIFAC, which was evolved with the help of 500 experts. In the last few years, there have been significant developments and technological revolutions. Now a consensus has emerged in all the sections of the society, particularly among the youth and children, to live in a Developed India and take appropriate actions. Even the Indian families living abroad have expressed their desire to participate in missions to transform India into a developed nation. In view of the above, a need has been felt to write this book. This book goes into the specific details pertaining to the impact of technology on society, and the missions leading to a Developed India by 2020.

When we were developing rockets, launch vehicles, missile systems and related technologies in India, the developed world denied technology, for many reasons, to us. This resulted in challenging the young minds into action. Technology denied is technology gained.

Today, India has core competence in system design, system engineering, system integration and system management of launch vehicles, missiles and aircraft, and capabilities for developing critical technologies. This book brings out these aspects in an integrated manner through two important case studies on the design of a launch vehicle and a guided missile.

Our aim is to convey that just like science, we have to make technology a universal system, decoupling geo-political policies. These case studies pertain to our experiences of working at ISRO and DRDO, and with great technology visionaries—Dr. Vikram Sarabhai and Prof. Satish Dhawan.

During the lectures and talks that have been given to school and college students participation of the youth has been tremendous and thought-provoking. It is these interactions with the youth of India that inspired us to share our experiences and vision in making India a developed nation.

India has many successful experiences of managing mission mode programmes. We recognise the importance of technology and the role that it can play while formulating policies and implementing programmes in mission mode. The requirement today is the creation of a suitable environment in tune with the times, and India's transformation into a knowledge society. For harnessing the potential of the youth and the resources, creative leadership is essential.

Networking of thoughts and deeds of one billion people towards a common goal of making India a developed nation is indeed the need of the hour.

A P J ABDUL KALAM

A SIVATHANU PILLAI

Acknowledgements

Many friends and associates from ISRO, DRDO, multiple scientific and academic institutions, TIFAC, other organisations and industry have provided inputs at various points of time, which have been used in writing this book. We are grateful to all of them.

In particularly, we are thankful to Shri G Sivakumar, for his help in the preparation of the lectures for the students of Anna University. Dr. A Kalanidhi, former Vice Chancellor of Anna University and Dr. E Balagurusamy, the present Vice Chancellor, for providing the opportunity to deliver a series of lectures on societal transformation to the students of various colleges of the University. Prof. K Udayakumar, Prof. Arun Balakrishnan and the faculty of computer engineering, biotech and other departments/centres of Anna University and the staff for providing support are gratefully acknowledged.

We would like to acknowledge the great efforts of Prof. P V Indiresan and Shri Y S Rajan for working out the details of PURA and technology requirements for Developed India. We would also like to thank Shri Prahlada and

Dr. B S Sarma for their contribution in writing an article in 1998, which became a reference for Case Study II. Shri Arun Tiwari, Shri R Swaminathan, the team of scientists from IISc, DRDO and BRAHMOS especially Dr. N Balakrishnan, Dr. M S Vijayaraghavan, Dr. W Selvamurthy, Shri K Srinivasa Rao, Shri P M Ajith, Shri Brij Mohan, Dr. Debashish Mukherji, Shri Mayank Dwivedi, Shri Sanjoy Mukherji, Shri V Ponraj Shri H Sheridon, Shri R K Prasad and Shri K Hariharan helped the authors in collating the content of the book. The authors would like to thank them all.

A P J ABDUL KALAM

A SIVATHANU PILLAI

Table of Contents

Abbreviations

ADA	Aeronautical Development Agency
AGV	Automated Guided Vehicle
AHWR	Advanced Heavy Water Reactors
AI	Artificial Intelligence
AIDS	Acquired Immune Deficiency Syndrome
ALH	Advanced Light Helicopter
AMH	Automated Materials Handling System
ASLV	Augmented Satellite Launch Vehicle
ASRS	Automated Storage and Retrieval System
ATM	Anti Tank Missile
B2B	Business to Business
B2C	Business to Consumer
BARC	Bhabha Atomic Research Centre
BWR	Boiling Water Reactors
CAD	Computer Aided Design
CADD	Computer Aided Design and Drafting
CAE	Computer Aided Engineering
CAM	Computer Aided Manufacturing
CAPP	Computer Aided Process Planning
CC	Carbon Carbon

CFC	Carbon Fibre Composite
CFD	Computational Fluid Dynamics
CIM	Computer Integrated Manufacturing
CNC	Computer Numerically Controlled
CODE	Components and Devices
CORE	Centre(s) Of Relevance & Excellence
CPT	Composite Product Technology
CPU	Central Processing Unit
CT Scan	Computed Tomography Scan
DAE	Department of Atomic Energy
DIPAS	Defence Institute of Physiology and Allied Sciences
DMRL	Defence Metallurgical Research Laboratory
DNA	Deoxyribo Nucleic Acid
DNC	Distributed Numerically Controlled
DRDL	Defence Research and Development Laboratory
DRDO	Defence Research and Development Organisation
EMI	Electro Magnetic Interference
ERP	Enterprise Resource Planning
FADECS	Full Authority Digital Engine Control System
FBR	Fast Breeder Reactors
FMS	Flexible Manufacturing System
FO	Fibre Optic
FRO	Floor Reaction Orthosis
FRP	Fibre Reinforced Plastic
FSAPDS	Fin Stabilised Armour Piercing and Discarding Sabot
FTC	Fin Tip Control
GDP	Gross Domestic Product
GEO	Geo Stationary Earth Orbit
GFLOPS	Giga Floating Point calculation per sec
GIS	Geographical Information System
GNP	Gross National Product
GSLV	Geo-synchronous Satellite Launch Vehicle
GT	Group Technology

GTO	Geo Transfer Orbit
HAL	Hindustan Aeronautics Limited
HAPP	Heavy Alloy Penetrator Plant
HILS	Hardware in loop simulation
HIV	Human Immunodeficiency Virus
HLLV	Heavy Lift Launch Vehicle
IC	Incubation Centres
ICAR	Indian Council of Agricultural Research
ICT	Information and Communication Technology
IDM	Individual Design Module
IFDB	Interface Design Module
IGCAR	Indira Gandhi Centre for Atomic Research
IGMDP	Integrated Guided Missile Development Programme
IIM	Indian Institute of Management
IIR	Imaging Infra Red
IISc	Indian Institute of Science
IIT	Indian Institute of Technology
IJT	Intermediate Jet Trainer
IMM	India Millennium Missions
INS	Inertial Navigation System
INSAT	Indian National Satellite
IPR	Intellectual Property Rights
IR	Infra Red
IRBM	Intermediate Range Ballistic Missile
IRS	Indian Remote Sensing
ISO	International Standards Organisation
ISRO	Indian Space Research Organisation
IT	Information Technology
ITES	Information Technology Enabled Services
JIT	Just in Time
LAVID	Launch Vehicle Integrated Design
LCA	Light Combat Aircraft
LEO	Low Earth Orbit
LPSC	Liquid Propulsion System Centre

LTA	Light Transport Aircraft
MBT	Main Battle Tank
MEMS	Micro-Electro Mechanical Systems
MIDHANI	Mishra Dhatu Nigam Limited
MIL Standards	Military Standards
MIU	Missile Interface Unit
MMIC	Microwave Monolithic Integrated Circuit
MP&CS	Manufacturing, Planning and Control Systems
MRI	Magnetic Resonance Imaging
MRP	Manufacturing Resource Planning
MTCR	Missile Technology Control Regime
NAL	National Aeronautical Laboratory
NC	Numerically Controlled
NEMS	Nano-Electro Mechanical Systems
NFTDC	Non-Ferrous Materials Technology Development Centre
NMRI	Nuclear Magnetic Resonance Imaging
NPC	Nuclear Power Corporation
NPOM	NPO Mashinostroyenia
PDS	Public Distribution System
PFBR	Prototype Fast Breeder Reactors
PHWR	Pressurised Heavy Water Reactors
PSLV	Polar Satellite Launch Vehicle
PURA	Providing Urban Amenities in Rural Areas
RCS	Reaction Control System
REACH	Relevance and Excellence in ACHieving new heights in education institutions
RLG	Ring Laser Gyro
SAC-C	Scientific Advisory Committee to the Cabinet
SAM	Surface to Air Missile
SASE	Snow and Avalanche Study Establishment
SBMT	Society for Biomedical Technology
SITAR	Society for Integrated Circuit Technology and Applied Research
SLV-3	Satellite Launch Vehicle
SPS	Solar Power Satellite

SSI	Small Scale Industries
TIFAC	Technology Information Forecasting Assessment Council
TIFR	Tata Institute of Fundamental Research
TVC	Thrust Vector Control
UAV	Unmanned Aerospace Vehicles
UDMH	Unsymmetrical Di-Methyl Hydrazine
VLSI	Very Large-Scale Integration
VR	Virtual Reality
VSAT	Very Small Aperture Terminal
VSSC	Vikram Sarabhai Space Centre

Introduction

If we turn the pages of history, we will know that India was a civilised and prosperous nation among the few in the world. The Indus Valley Civilisation and the ruins of Mohenjo-Daro and Harappa bear testimony to the fact that even as early as 2500 B.C., India had developed the skills for agriculture, pottery, tools, jewellery, artifacts and metal alloy idols. Later, around the 6th century B.C., the Magadh Empire saw the birth of cities and the use of coins. Subsequently, the Mauryan period saw texts like *Arthasastra* written by Kautilya. Under King Ashoka, prosperity and progress continued and the Mauryan empire spread its rule far and wide.

From time to time India, however, faced successive invasions from foreign rulers, which became an impediment to its development. The country missed the Industrial Revolution, that transformed the West as an economic power. Coupled with increasing population, famine and poverty, India, which was once a prosperous nation, was reduced to subjugation and penury by successive foreign rulers.

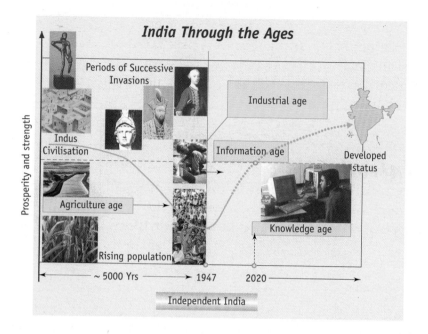

The first vision of Independence in 1857 triggered the process of change. Later the freedom movement brought the best of leaders in politics, public life, music, poetry, literature and science. This movement was driven by patriotism and sacrifice with an unity of mind and purpose. There was a desire in many Indians to excel and surpass foreigners in every field of life. This led to many Indians demonstrating their individual talent. In *Chandra*, the biography of the famous astrophysicist S Chandra Sekhar by Kameshwar Wali, it reads "Before 1910 there were no Indian scientist of international reputation, but after the First World War, between 1920 and 1925, suddenly five scientists of international reputation emerged. They were J C Bose, C V Raman, Megnath Saha, Srinivasa Ramanujan, and Prof. Chandra Sekhar himself. I have associated this remarkable phenomenon with the need for self-expression, which became a dominant motive among the young during the National Movement. It was a part of the National Movement to assert oneself. We could show the West in their own realm, that we were equal to them." Like science, the first vision of the freedom movement generated top-class leaders in every walk of life.

Now India has a large human resource with skill and endurance. Large-scale development of human resource came into being because of the structured five-year plans by the government and focused mission mode programmes. Still the current GDP growth rate is only 4.5%, the population below the poverty level is 26%, and unemployment is 30%. This situation needs a change. A positive movement can come only from a second vision for the nation's development, i.e. Developed India by 2020.

Fortunately, with the advent of the knowledge age, India finds itself in a very advantageous position as it will bring societal transformation in education, healthcare, agriculture and governance. This transformation will lead to large employment generation, high productivity, high national growth, empowerment of the weaker sections, networked and transparent society and rural prosperity. India's glory will again return during the knowledge age, as India has the core competencies of information and communication technologies and knowledge workers. Our strength is to be capitalised to achieve the above goals of nation building.

The importance of technology in nation building is the triggering point for writing this book. The book presents a strategic view of technology capabilities and discusses a few critical areas in the Indian context like design and manufacturing, the strategic sector, agriculture and the healthcare sector. The book aims to stimulate discussions leading to concrete actions on harnessing the emerging technologies for empowering india.

Divided into eight chapters, the book deals with specific aspects of technology:

- The first chapter deals with the influence of technology and its impact on human life. It discusses the Second Vision for India in the form of a developed nation by 2020 and the thrust areas identified by Technology Vision 2020

- The second chapter examines the various dimensions of technology like specification, design, manufacturing, etc., and the important role of indigenous design in technology development

- The next four chapters discuss the influence of technology in the areas of agriculture, manufacturing, healthcare and strategic sectors.

- The seventh chapter discusses the evolution of the knowledge society and India's core competence in becoming a knowledge economy.

- The eighth chapter identifies the actions needed to transform India from a developing country to a developed nation.

This book brings out the role and importance of technology for the nation's development and is presented here as a roadmap which will benefit students and youth to contribute in achieving missions leading to Developed India. It also identifies the role of Indians working in fields like design, manufacturing, healthcare, agriculture, education, law, information and communication technology, administration and so on. Also, the book will be of interest to the great Indian family, including NRIs and NGOs for participating in Nation building.

1

Technology: The Prime Mover for a Developed Nation

INTRODUCTION

Technology has had a profound influence on human civilisation and will continue to do so in the future too. This chapter examines the areas where technology will have an impact, in the backdrop of factors, like the changing pattern of energy consumption and the advent of a knowledge society. The Second Vision for India in the form of a Developed Nation by 2020 and the areas requiring thrust, as identified by Technology Vision 2020, have been discussed in this chapter.

Prof. Kalam with students at Anna University

> **"** Learning gives creativity
> Creativity leads to thinking
> Thinking provides knowledge
> Knowledge makes you great **"**

GROWTH OF TECHNOLOGY AND ITS IMPACT ON HUMANITY

After about 1,00,000 millennia of existence, our ancestors developed stone tools for hunting. As can be seen from Table 1.1, it was 3500 years ago that they could develop marine transport. In the last 200 years, with the advent of the industrial revolution, inventions like the railways and electricity came into being. Major innovations like the aircraft, mass-produced chemical products, nuclear weapons, and computers have now been accomplished. In the last few decades, the rate of invention and development has grown exponentially, as reflected in the emergence of the Internet, improved communication tools, and genetically engineered plants. Figure 1.1 shows the growth of technology and its impact on humanity.

Technological strength is the key to creating productive employment in an increasingly competitive market place and to continually upgrade human skills. By the pervasive use of technologies, we can achieve a holistic development of our people in the years to come.

Table 1.1

Approximate time (years preceding 2002)	Innovation/ breakthrough	Consequence/ reason
1,00,000	Making and using stone gear for hunting	Extending human capabilities
40,000	Making and using weapons	Extending human capabilities
3,500	Boats and sailboats	Extending human capabilities
800	Clock, compass, and other measurement instruments	Reduced and/or simplified manual work
360	Mechanical calculators	Replacing human computation
190	Railways (using coal and oil for energy)	Facilitating and/or making mental work easier
160	Electricity	Improving quality of life
140	Image and sound reproduction	Providing entertainment and spread of knowledge
100	Telecommunications and X-rays	Improving comfort and/or speed of communication
95	Automobiles and roads	Increased speed and/or availability of telecommunications
80	Aircraft	Faster travel
70	Mass-produced chemicals	Improving quality of treatment and other allied areas
55	Nuclear weapons/energy	Extending human capabilities
50	Computers	Improving the quality of life
45	Mass-produced home appliances	Improving the material quality of life
40	Fertilisers and oral contraceptives	Improving quality of life
35	Lasers	Extending human capabilities
30	The moon landing, tissues, and organ transplants	Extending human capabilities
20	The CT (CAT or Body) scan	Improvement in diagnostic tools
10	Genetically engineered plants, Internet	Increased knowledge base

Adapted from *"Forecasting, Planning and Strategy, for the 21st Century"*, Makrindakis Sproys G., (© Penguin Books India Pvt. Ltd.)

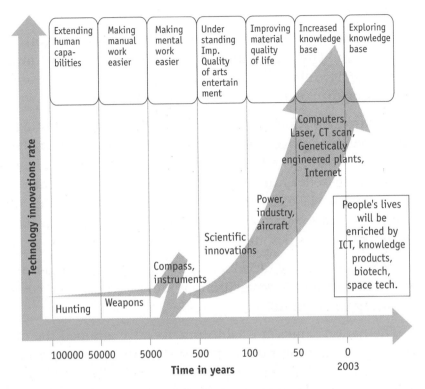

Fig. 1.1 *Growth of Technologies and Human Impact*

CAN TECHNOLOGY TRANSFORM INDIA INTO A DEVELOPED NATION?

India, after its Independence, was determined to move ahead towards growth, development and prosperity with the help of planned policies for science and technology. Now, more than five decades later the scenario is quite different.

Within two decades of the birth of nuclear science in India, nuclear medicine, nuclear irradiation for preservation of agricultural products, nuclear power and much later nuclear weapons were developed.

The nation is self-sufficient in food production, making the near-famine conditions of the 1950s a long-forgotten nightmare. The developments in the health sector and medicine have eliminated quite a few contagious diseases and have brought about an increase in life expectancy.

Today, small-scale industries contribute a high percentage to the national gross domestic product (GDP)—a vast change in the 1990s compared to the 1950s. In recent times, we have also witnessed impressive growth in the Information Technology (IT) sector—the country is progressing in hardware and software export business which are more than 10 billion dollars despite the ebb in the last few years.

India is designing, developing, and launching world-class geostationary and sun-synchronous remote sensing and communication satellites.

The nation's nuclear establishments have attained the capability of building nuclear power stations, developing nuclear medicine, and undertaking nuclear irradiation of agricultural seeds for enhanced agricultural production. Within two decades of the birth of nuclear science in India, nuclear medicine, nuclear irradiation for preservation of agricultural products, nuclear power, and much later, nuclear weapons were created.

Innovative defence research has led to the design, development, and production of main battle tanks, advanced missile systems, light combat aircraft, electronic warfare systems, and various armours. Figure 1.2 indicates this advancement. Today, India has many advanced technology systems. Yet India is a developing country. What more can technology do?

Technology has multiple dimensions. Geopolitics can facilitate the adaptation of technology to a nation's needs, which can lead to economic prosperity and also reinforce

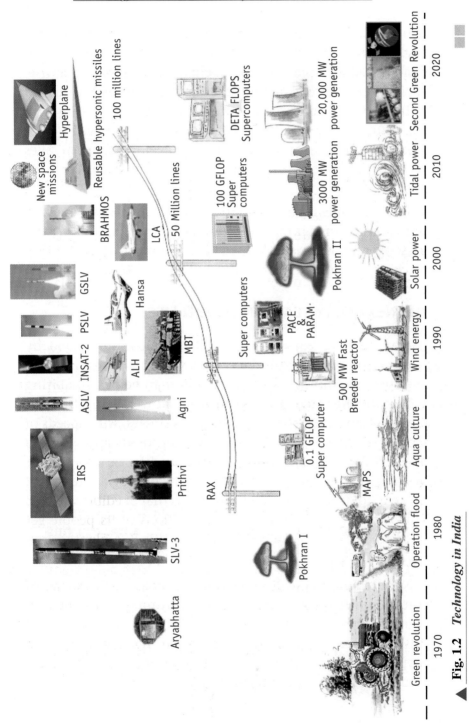

Fig. 1.2 *Technology in India*

national security. For example, the developments in chemical engineering created fertilisers for higher crop yield but also contributed to the production of chemical weapons. Likewise, rocket technology developed for atmospheric research helped in launching satellites for remote sensing and communication, which are vital for the economic development. The same technology led to the development of missiles with specific defence capabilities that provide security to the nation.

The advancements in aviation technology have enabled the creation of fighter and bomber aircraft, as well as the passenger jet. These also helped in relief operations, by swiftly reaching support to people affected by disasters.

THE NEXT FIFTY YEARS IN HUMAN LIFE

In the coming years, peoples lives will be enriched by IT-driven knowledge products and systems, biotechnology, and space technology. We may find human-beings inhabiting a planet other than earth and solar power being beamed down to earth. Moreover, hypersonic vehicles, with speeds of more than Mach 10, will fly across continents and will also be used for weapons delivery. Human life will be further prolonged through genomic and biotechnological research. An area holding even greater promise is that of edible vaccine. This would be a boon to India as millions of its people get affected by diseases like Polio and Hepatitis-B. A plant system for delivering the vaccine needs to be developed.

Nanotechnology will enter human usage in the shape of control mechanisms of various transporting systems, medical equipment, and aerospace systems like micro-satellites, mini RPV. Another area of human concern in the coming decades would be the pattern of global energy dependence. Figure 1.3 indicates the technology for the next fifty years.

In the coming decades, we may see the birth of a unified field theory, integrating gravitional forces, electro-magnetic forces, general relativity theory, space, and time as functions.

With this background, the economic growth in different societies—past and present—is discussed in the following paragraphs.

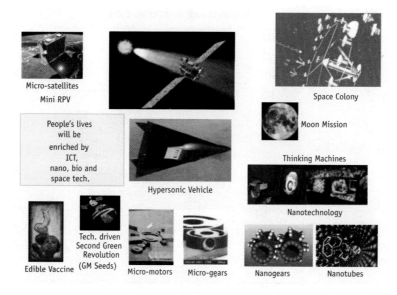

▲ **Fig. 1.3** *Technology for the Next Fifty Years*

Economic Scenario

Let us begin by first examining India's economic situation relative to other great powers of the world. We notice that in the last decade India's rate of growth has been significantly high coinciding as it did with economic liberalisation. What is significant is that our rate of growth is much higher than that of many other countries.

While India is moving ahead faster in terms of absolute gross domestic product, among, USA, Germany and Japan,

USA is pre-eminent in terms of wealth. It is not our aim to fantasise that we should catch up and overtake America within the next decade or so. What we need to do is to take responsibility for our own well-being and develop our society consistent with our heritage and sense of value and capability. We need to aim very high and work for it.

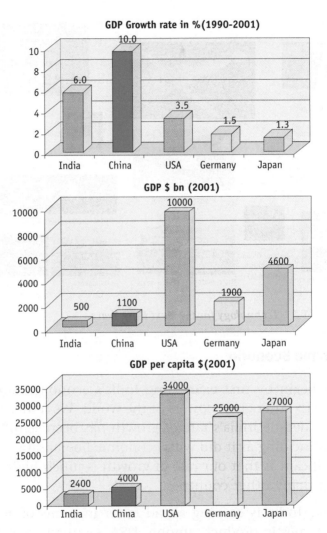

▲   **Fig. 1.4   *India's Position in the World Economic Scenario***

Another economic indicator is Gross Domestic Product per capita. Compared to China, our GDP per capita is lower (Fig. 1.4). The main reasons for this was the delay in starting the development process. China started development process atleast a decade earlier and their investment was much higher. This should be a concern for us as nearly 70% of our population lives in about 580,000 villages spread all over the country and while the benefits of economic growth have been felt in urban areas to a large extent. Productivity in rural areas is very low, thus economic conditions need improvement. We should aim at a high level of prosperity, facility and infrastructure in the rural areas keeping intact the pure environment of the rural areas.

Therefore, our basic strategy for social and economic transformation of India towards its vision as developed society by 2020, would be a strong focus on providing urban amenities in rural areas in a most creative and cost effective manner. This is the challenge in front of the country and it need the contribution of our great Indian family not only within the border of India but also spread all over the world, in terms of knowledge, expertise, business acumen and management skills to start a well-synchronised economic revolution through well-conceived missions, strategies, goals and policies.

It is important now to identify the fundamental sectoral contributors to GDP of different countries. By this study we will understand how the advanced countries have transformed themselves to an era of prosperity and strength.

It would be seen that in the most prosperous of these nations such as the USA, Germany and Japan, the greatest contributors to national wealth are the service sector and manufacturing. However, in China and India the agricultural sector is dominant due to their vast population (Fig. 1.5). While agriculture is important, its value creation has limitations.

India's consumption of food would double by 2020, whereas the land available for cultivation would further reduce. It means that with lesser area, and lesser water, India has to double the production only by technology and farm management. It is came with manufacturing, though it can absorb more people in productive jobs than the agricultural sector.

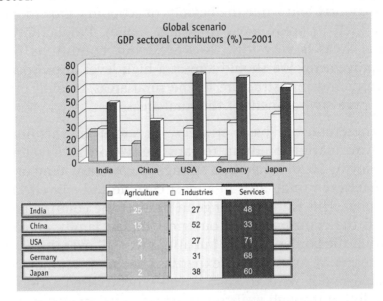

Global scenario
GDP sectoral contributors (%)—2001

	Agriculture	Industries	Services
India	25	27	48
China	15	52	33
USA	2	27	71
Germany	1	31	68
Japan	2	38	60

▲   **Fig. 1.5   *GDP Sectoral Contributors—Global Scenario***

Economic Growth in Different Societies

During the 20th century, societies underwent a change—from the agricultural society, where manual labour was the critical factor—to the industrial society, where the management of technology, capital, and labour provided the competitive advantage. The information era was born in the last decade —connectivity and software products drove the economies of a few nations. In the 21st century, a new society is emerging—knowledge is the primary production resource instead of capital or labour.

Efficient utilisation of existing knowledge can create a comprehensive wealth for the nation and also improve the quality of life, in the form of better health, education, infrastructure, and other social indicators. The ability to create and maintain a knowledge

Efficient utilisation of existing knowledge can create a comprehensive wealth for the nation and also improve the quality of life, in the form of better health, education, infrastructure, and other social indicators.

society infrastructure, develop the knowledge of workers, and enhance their productivity through the creation, growth, and exploitation of new knowledge, will be the key factor in deciding the prosperity of this knowledge society. Whether or not a nation has developed into a knowledge society is judged by the way it creates and deploys knowledge in the sectors like IT, industry, agriculture, healthcare, and so on. Economic growth in different socities is depicted in Fig. 1.6.

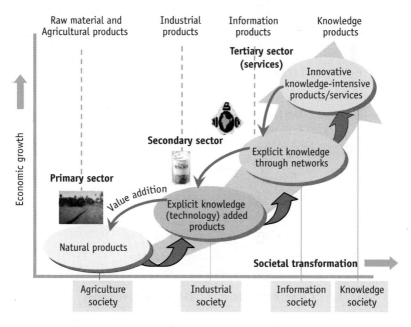

Fig. 1.6 *Economic Growth in Different Societies*

CHANGE IN EMPLOYMENT—AGRICULTURE, INDUSTRY, AND SERVICE-KNOWLEDGE INDUSTRIES

Whether or not a nation has developed into a knowledge society is judged by the way it creates and deploys knowledge in the sectors like IT, industry, agriculture, healthcare, and so on.

In the 1980s, the agriculture sector employed—partially or fully—70% of the people of the country. This figure reduced to 65% by 1994 and is expected to further fall to 60% by 2012. However, because the demand for agricultural products will double, increased productivity through technology and efficient post-harvest management will have to compensate for the manpower reduction in the farming and agricultural products sectors.

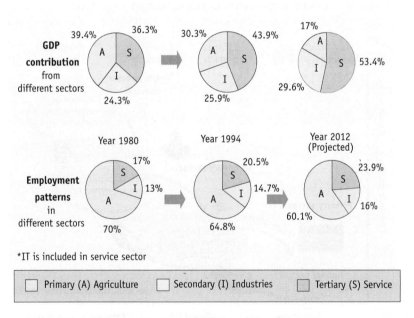

Fig. 1.7　*Changing Pattern of GDP and Employment*

In the case of industry, in the 1980s, 13% of the population was employed in small- and large-scale industries. The trend continued till 1994. However, it is expected to increase to 16% in 2012 and the pattern of employment will take a new shape, with high technology use and the opening-up of the economy under the WTO. Changing pattern of GDP and employment are shown in Fig. 1.7.

It is seen that the service industry, with a knowledge component, has risen in employability from 17% in 1980 to 20% in 1994, and will further increase to around 24% by 2012 due to the demands from the sectors of infrastructure, maintenance, finance, IT, and entertainment.

This big change will require trained and skilled human resources and technology personnel in all areas. Our industrialists, commercial chiefs, and technologists may have to get ready for such transformations in agriculture, industries, and the service-knowledge sector, for which manpower with knowledge and skills needs to be evolved in a mission mode.

From the above, we can realise that the GDP growth and additional employment potential can come only through a well defined strategy for development. This is possible if the nation has a vision.

VISION FOR THE NATION

The first vision of India was seeded in 1857 for freedom, which culminated in 1947, after 90 years of sacrifice and struggle. This vision created excellent leaders in diverse fields like politics, philosophy, science, technology, and industry.

Also improvements took place in many aspects of life, like literacy, agriculture, strategic areas, and small and large-scale industries. Now, more than 50 years have gone by after Independence and we are yet among one of the hundreds of developing countries, distinct from the G-8 countries. Indeed, we have many challenges. This resulted in envisioning the Developed India by 2020 (Fig. 1.8). Experts pooled their ideas and evolved Technology Vision 2020.

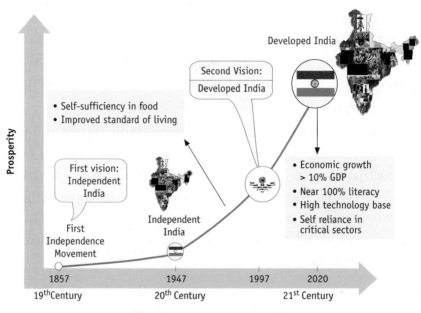

▲   **Fig. 1.8   *Emerging India***

TIFAC STUDY ON TECHNOLOGY VISION 2020

A developed country, in our opinion, is one that has the capability and the capacity to comprehensively look at wealth generation and national security, and thereafter evolve integrated strategies, technologies, and missions to meet these objectives. It is also a fact that technology is the established currency of geopolitical power and, in the Indian context, technology has to be the driving force for the economic development and national security.

In recognition of the above reality, two documents have been prepared by two different streams of national experts: Technology Information Forecasting Assessment Council (TIFAC) an autonomous body under the Department of Science and Technology, and the Department of Defence Research and Development. These are *Technology Vision 2020* in 17 volumes (Fig. 1.9) and *Integrated Strategies, Technologies and Missions for Comprehensive National Security*. These two documents have addressed the aspects of wealth generation in a comprehensive manner and identified technology as the linking factor. The fusion of these two documents has resulted in *IMM (India Millennium Missions) 2020*, which provides an excellent framework and a roadmap for creating a strong and developed India by the year 2020.

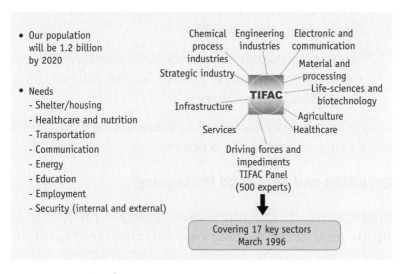

▲ **Fig. 1.9 *Technology Vision—2020***

INTEGRATED ACTION FOR DEVELOPED INDIA

Five areas have been indentified, based on India's core competence, for integrated action:

1. **Agriculture and agro-food processing:** A target of 360 million tonnes of food and agricultural production per annum is aimed at. Agriculture and agro-food processing would bring prosperity to the rural people and speed-up the economic growth.

2. **Education and healthcare:** Experience proves that education and healthcare are interrelated and assist in healthy life and population control, leading to social security.

3. **Information and communication technology:** This area can be used effectively to promote education in remote areas and also to create national wealth.

4. **Infrastructure, including electric power:** Crucial for overall development, reliable and quality electric power for all parts of the country.

5. **Strategic industries and critical technology:** This area, fortunately, witnessed growth in the Nuclear, Space, and Defence Technologies.

The development of core sectors as identified have their impact on the other sectors of the economy.

Agriculture and Agro-food Processing

Improvements in agriculture and agro-food processing can lead to food security, employment and rapid economic growth. We have to target a doubling of the present production of food and agricultural products. Other areas of agriculture and agro-food processing would bring prosperity to rural people and speed-up the economic growth.

India is poised for the Second Green Revolution using the advantages of biotechnology, appropriate seed selection, soil characterisation, post-harvest management, food processing and marketing. Better storage facilities are required to avoid the loss, we must also ensure fast distribution system, so that the products can reach the needy people.

India is the largest milk producer in the world having a production of 78 million MT generating a business of $13.6 billion per year. India has the largest population of cattle in the world at 33 million. But in, terms of productivity, it ranks 54th mainly on account of poor cattle hygiene and healthcare practices. The adoption of proper cattle management and adoption of cold chains, proper containerisation, aseptic packaging and electronic testing machines can lead to an increase in the production of milk to 300 million MT, generating business of $67 billion by the year 2020. There is a need for many food processing industries.

Education and Healthcare

Education is the pillar of a strong and developed nation. In the knowledge society, intellectual capacity will dominate. Therefore, education must become a thrust area, aimed at 100% literacy. This is the key for employment. Women's education is particularly important to bring societal transformation, including small family, higher education and better healthcare for children.

We have seen that education and healthcare are inter-related. Many diseases can be brought under control by the adoption of proper health and hygiene, preventive health-care systems like inoculation, vaccination, immunisation, periodic health checks and medical treatment. Further, the invention of vaccines, increasing use of natural products and new techniques like genetic engineering and rapid diagnostics will lead to "Health for All" by the year 2020.

Information and Communication Technology

IT is one of the core areas where India has an expertise and competitive edge. The significant contribution of India's economic growth comes from this sector. The software and service industries now account for 16% of the country's overall exports, an employment of five lakh professionals and $1.5 billion in investment. It is expected that there will be further growth in Information Technology particularly in IT Enabled Services (ITES) from off-shore companies leading to rapid economic growth, increase in export earnings and massive employment opportunities. To sustain the growth in software industry, one has to think of newer strategies. So far, software development in the country has been concentrated in selected cities like Bangalore, Delhi, Hyderabad, Pune, Chennai, etc. It is yet to percolate down to smaller cities and towns. Rural information networks can allow knowledge services, transactions and certain kinds of products to flow more easily across long distances.

In order to take full advantage of the technological developments, investments in communication area have to be made. Rapid expansion and extension of India's fixed and mobile telecom infrastructure is essential for stimulating growth in this sector. Other areas which can be concentrated upon in the IT sector include information security, e-governance, software development, entertainment, education, hardware development, etc. The Indian IT industry must become the leading MNC's in the world. From the meagre target of $88 billion by 2008, Indian IT industry must aim $140 billion, to have edge.The industry is also expected to generate a total employment of four million persons accounting for 7% of India's GDP and 30% of foreign exchange inflow by the year 2008.

IT would become a potent tool in integrating the nation. The remote localities that are now feeling a sense of neglect will no longer feel so. Time and distance will be shortened to make the world's largest democracy an efficient, competitive and dynamic nation.

The future challenges in Information Technology include the issues related to software security. Open source codes can easily introduce the users to build security algorithms in the system. Indian software industry still seems to believe in proprietary solutions. Further, the spread of IT which is influencing the daily life of individuals. It would have a devastating effect on the lives of society due to any small shift in the business practice involving these proprietary solutions. It is precisely for these reasons, open source software needs to be built which would be cost effective for the entire society and would provide the necessary security. In India, open source code software will have to come and stay in a big way for the benefit of our billion people.

Infrastructure, including Electric Power

Infrastructure is crucial for all areas which include agriculture, Information Technology, healthcare and strategic industries. For economic prosperity, stress needs to be provided on rural infrastructure as there is a disparity between the facilities existing in urban and rural areas. It has been estimated that the soaring demand for power will necessitate a tripling of the installed generation capacity from 100,000 MW to 300,000 MW over the next two decades. 80000 villages are yet to get electricity connections and quite a few of them are in remote areas where conventional electricity grid may not be feasible. Therefore, in rural areas, non-conventional energy sources like biomass, wind and solar power needs to be adopted. The infrastructure development is also required in the telecommunication area, which will help in the growth of Information Technology.

Two other important missions, Networking of Rivers and Providing Urban Amenities in Rural Areas (PURA), are discussed in Chapter 8—Vision to Mission.

Strategic Industries and Critical Technologies

India has emerged as a strong nation in the area of strategic industries inspite of the sanctions and control regimes like Missile Technology Control Regime. Achievements have come in the form of space missions like Geosynchronous Satellite Launch Vehicle (GSLV), Strategic and Cruise missiles, Aeronautical systems like Light Combat Aircraft (Tejas), Intermediate Jet Trainer (IJT), Advanced Light Helicopter (ALH). Major programmes were undertaken during the last decade by Defence Research and Development Organisation like Main Battle Tank (MBT) *Arjun*, Missiles *Prithvi*, *Agni* and BRAHMOS, Pilot-less Target Aircraft *Lakshya*, and many others. Due to the various aerospace programmes several technologies were developed, notable among them include computational fluid dynamics, development of silicon and gallium arsenide foundries for VLSI and MMIC components, solid and liquid propulsion in the case of Space, Missile and LCA programmes, and digital fly-by-wire control system in the case of LCA. In the sphere of composite technology the carbon–carbon nose tip of *Agni,* low loss radomes and composite wings of LCA were significant developments. The technologies so developed in the strategic sectors have the capabilities to augment the technological strengths in other industries, thus leading to economic prosperity.

The sectors discussed, i.e., education and healthcare, agriculture and agro-food processing, Information Technology, infrastructure and strategic industries can together lead to the strengthening of the economy and the nation's security. With the integrated actions in the above areas it is expected that the GDP growth rate will climb up from 4.5% to more than 10%, and the people below the poverty line to almost near zero.

These five areas are closely interlinked and will lead to national food, economic, and strategic security. A strong partnership among the R&D sector, academia, industry, business, the community as a whole, and government departments and agencies will be essential to accomplish the vision. The links are shown in Fig. 1.10.

VISION, MISSION AND GOALS

Deliberations of the task force on Technology Vision 2020 recommend the coupling of core strengths of the nation with the desired goals. The nation's strengths predominantly reside in its natural and human resources.

> *The nation's strengths predominantly reside in its natural and human resources.*

India is endowed with a vast coastline with marine resources and also oil wealth. Apart from conventional mineral resources, it is well-known that India has the largest deposits of titanium, beryllium, and tungsten. India ranks among the world's leading mega biodiverse nations. In the herbal area particularly, there are potential applications for developing multiple products for nutrition and cure of diseases. Currently, of the global herbal product market of 61 billion dollars, China has a share of around 3 billion dollars, whereas India's share is not even 100 million dollars. Hence, there is tremendous opportunity for growth in this area. India has similar potential for promoting floriculture and aquaculture in a big way. Knowledge-based value addition for these natural resources would mean exporting value-added products rather than merely the raw materials.

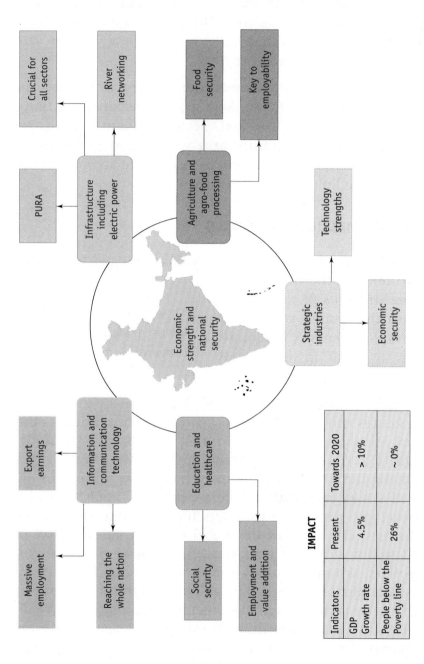

IMPACT

Indicators	Present	Towards 2020
GDP Growth rate	4.5%	> 10%
People below the Poverty line	26%	~ 0%

▲ **Fig. 1.10** *Integrated Action for Developed India*

The use of IT for commercialisation and marketing can increase our reach and speed enormously. Figure 1.11 depicts the vision, mission and goals for India for 2020.

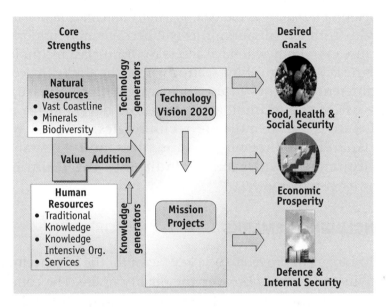

▲   **Fig. 1.11**   *Vision, Mission and Goals*

Our ancient knowledge is a unique resource, for it holds the treasure of nearly 5000 years of civilisation. It is essential to leverage this wealth for ensuring national well-being as also for creating a rightful place for the nation in the global map.

Human resource, particularly the large population of youth, is a unique core strength of the nation. This resource can be strengthened through various educational and training programmes. Skilled, un-skilled, and creative man-power can be transformed into wealth generators particularly in the service

Human resource, particularly the large population of youth, is a unique core strength of the nation.

sectors and agro-industries. Knowledge-intensive industries can be generated out of existing ones by injecting the demand for high-level software and hardware, which would bring tremendous value addition. It is said, *'The precious asset of a company or a country is the skill, ingenuity and imagination of its people'.* With globalisation, this will become more important because everybody will have access to world-class technology and the key distinguishing feature will be the ability of people in different countries to use their imagination to make the best use of the technology. Indeed, the development and innovative use of multiple technologies, coupled with transparent management structures and IT-enabled environments, will catapult India into the realm of a knowledge superpower.

CONCLUDING REMARKS

Technology has proved to be a key factor for the advancement of civilisation and improving the quality of life. The coming years will see technology dominating all walks of life. India is committed to become a developed nation by the year 2020 and technology will play a dominant role. The Technology Vision 2020 documents have already identified the areas where thrust is required for realising the vision. India should leave no stone unturned to fully exploit its core strengths, in the form of natural and human resources, in realising the vision.

India is committed to become a developed nation by the year 2020 and technology will play a dominant role.

We have seen and worked with creators of visions and missions. A strong vision ignites the young minds. Let us recall the saying of Maharishi Patanchali in *Yogasuthra.*

"When you are inspired by some great purpose, some extraordinary project, all your thoughts break their bounds. Your mind transcends

limitations, your consciousness expands in every direction, and you find yourself in a new, great, and wonderful world. Dormant forces, faculties, and talents come alive, and you discover yourself to be a greater person by far than you ever dreamt yourself to be."

Let this saintly saying enter into the minds and transform the youth of India to toil for creating 'Developed India' in two decades. Technology is the prime mover for achieving the vision. Let us therefore discuss the dimensions of technology.

The Dimensions
of Technology

INTRODUCTION

Technology encompasses various dimensions like requirement specifications, design, process, manufacturing, servicing and product improvement. Out of these, in the value-chain of a product, design adds value of over 60%. This chapter emphasises this aspect and presents examples related to the design and manufacturing of a few high technology aerospace projects in India. The chapter concludes with the message that indigenous design capability provides a competitive edge to the nation.

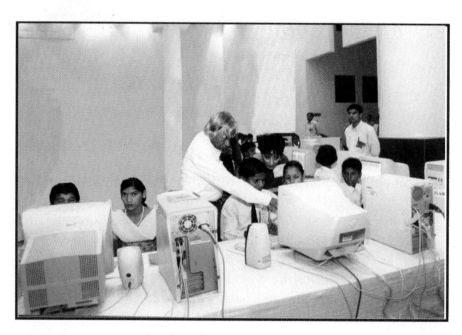

Prof. Kalam interacting with students

" ** Technology is a non-linear tool that can effect the most fundamental change in the ground rules of economic competitiveness **"

TECHNOLOGY: DEFINITION

Technology is the confluence of multiple scientific disciplines, tested and proven and put to use for a nation's prosperity. Technology can also be defined as the maturity of scientific discovery for multiple applications.

Of course, there is a time lag between a scientific discovery and the development of applications. In the electronics and communication fields, it takes less than five years for a discovery to become an application, while it takes about ten years in material and manufacturing fields and even more time in some fields like pharmaceuticals, etc.

TECHNOLOGY INTERFACES

1. Technology is a non-linear tool that can bring about the most fundamental change in the ground rules of economic competitiveness.
   - Science is linked to technology through applications.
   - Technology is linked to economy and environment through the manufacturing processes.
   - Economy and environment link technology to the society.

2. As depicted in Fig. 2.1, the integrated relationship of science, technology, economy, environment, manufacturing, and the society is evident.

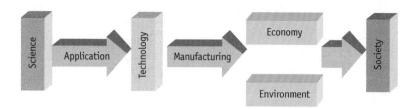

▲　**Fig. 2.1**　*Technology Interfaces*

THE GENERAL ECONOMIC CYCLE OF A TECHNOLOGY

The general characterisation of the technology cycle commences with R&D to the market growth pattern leading to technology displacement and obsolescence. The actual timing and valuations depend upon the particular technology and the market it serves. Examples of short life cycles include computers, dial-up modems and microprocessors, and also much of the underlying semiconductor manufacturing

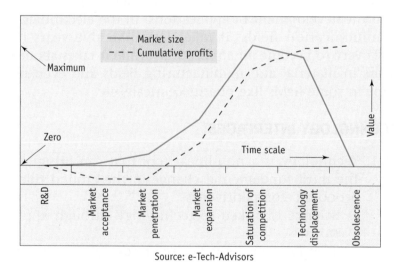

Source: e-Tech-Advisors

▲　**Fig. 2.2**　*General Economic Cycle of a Technology*

technology. Internal combustion engines, traditional telephone voice networks, and aircraft represent examples of technologies with relatively long life cycles. The message is clear—technology and economic cycle have to be dynamic and should assess the potential of the market as the customers want change (Fig. 2.2).

THRUST FOR INDIGENOUS TECHNOLOGY

Technology consists of stages like research and development, technology transfer, technology absorption, and production of products or systems with the desired performance, quality, and cost-effectiveness.

Technology development can be achieved through two routes—Route A and Route B. Route A (know-how) involves obtaining licensed technology or techniques including manufacturing, design drawings, and production processes from an established manufacturer from abroad.

Route B (know-why) begins with designing and developing indigenous technology. In the case of India, progress in technology, particularly indigenous design, is the thrust area to enable India to become competitive with other countries. The strength of indigenous technology is highlighted in Fig. 2.3.

To be competitive within India and in the global market, it is essential to evolve a value-chain in a product life cycle. In Fig. 2.4, value-chain is provided for the wealth generation and quality improvement in percentages. It can be seen that among specifications/requirement, design, process, manufacturing, services, and product improvement, wealth generation depends largely on the design strength, which requires 60% of the product life cycle effort. The figure also brings out that the quality has to be built-in at an optimal level during the design phase itself (quantitatively about

40%). For a product value-chain, largely design effort with built-in quality influences the competitiveness of the product.

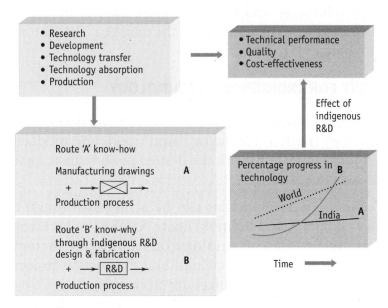

▲   **Fig. 2.3   *Indigenous Research and Development (R&D)***

Based on the experiences gained in launch vehicles and guided missiles, India has the competitive edge to design and develop any type of launch vehicle, missile, military aircraft and reusable system. With the partnership of Indian academic institutions, industry and different R&D departments, we can definitely see the tremendous strength India has in critical sectors. We have included two important case studies in the later part of the book. The first case study (I) pertains to the design methodology of Satellite Launch Vehicle (SLV- 3) and the second study pertains to the design of a complex surface-to-air missile. These case studies will enthuse

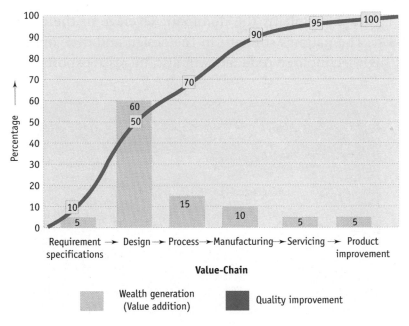

Fig. 2.4 *Evolution of the Value-Chain in a Product Life Cycle*

our younger generation to understand India's capability to carry out complex aerospace designs with an integrated approach. This also establishes that India has the capability for systems design, systems engineering and systems integration of rockets, missiles and launch vehicles. This capability has provided the necessary impetus for the production and marketing of aerospace systems to the customers delight.

Indigenous design and development capabilities are the keys to gaining a competitive edge. The competitive edge is governed by low-cost, high-quality and superior performance, and timeliness, that will bring customers delight which is a function of design and development, manufacturing and service.

> *Indigenous design and development capabilities are the keys to gaining a competitive edge.*

Figure 2.5 explains the dominant leverage of the design effort. The nation's strength in the design and development of high technology products will also increase exports.

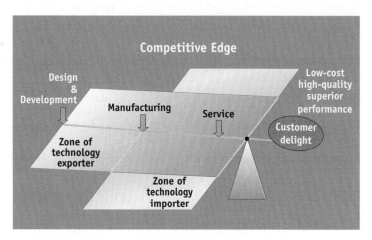

Fig. 2.5   *Indigenous Design and Development Capability*

It is therefore important that the Indian R&D sector, business people, and industries recognise this dimension of technology.

Indigenous design and development, and manufacturing experiences are highlighted in the following sections, using examples on rocket motor casing, magnesium wings for *Prithvi, Vikas* engine and solid booster motor casing for PSLV, *Kaveri* combuster, titanium air bottles for LCA, and onboard computers for flight system used in launch vehicle/missile systems. Practices applied and adopted in these examples will be common to most of the product manufacturing industries, as the design and manufacturing practices of space and defence technology comply to ISO standards.

(a) FRP Rocket Motor Case: Design and Manufacturing

In the third stage of developing a launch vehicle rocket system, Composite Product Technology (CPT) was selected to design a light structure with high strength for a rocket motor casing, which houses the solid propellant—the source of the energy provider of a rocket.

To make a light rocket motor casing, inputs are required in the area of reinforcement such as fibre glass roving or carbon fibre, binders like epoxy varieties, and design methodology and processes. The design itself uses conventional and Computer-Aided Design (CAD) involving hundreds of man-hours.

With these inputs, the Fibre Reinforced Plastic motor casing has a unique design and fabrication feature—a directionally reinforced structure to provide the required strength, an advantage of composites compared to metal alloys. Automated filament winding machine built indigenously, facilitates the winding of wet fibres at a particular angle with viscosity control. Fabrication methodology was evolved for the integration of metallic fittings for the payload on one side of the motor casing and the nozzle on the other side (Fig. 2.6).

The thickness of the motor case has to be designed suitably, keeping safety in mind and has to be fabricated with the filament wound process. Also during the winding operation a high temperature liner has to be embedded inside the motor case and the mandrel of the winding operation has to be of a collapsible type. Quality control and check is very important, particularly in the reinforcement of the fibre epoxy binder and viscosity control during the winding to keep the binder in proportion to the reinforcement (the binder has to be less than 40% by weight for optimum strength of the structure).

The composite motor case thus built has to be hydraulically tested to withstand operational pressure.

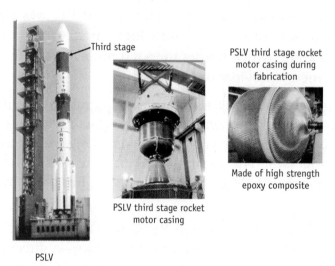

▲   **Fig. 2.6   *Composite Rocket Motor***

A successful rocket case emerges due to the right selection of material and machinery as well as controlled temperature during the manufacturing process. It is this integration of a multiple fields of engineering that leads to a single value-added product.

Hence, composite product technology has become futuristic in structural sub-system and systems design and development. High specific strength material is essential in every field, such as automobiles or water transportation tanks.

(b) PSLV Booster Motor Case

The manufacture of the booster motor casing for the first stage of PSLV was a challenging job as the motor case had a diameter of 2.8 m for holding 125 tonnes of solid propellant. Another challenge was the use of maraging steel, an alloy steel with high strength as well as high fracture toughness as compared to other alloys like 15CDV6. With the successful use of this material, it was possible to make the walls of the casing thinner without compromising the casing's ability to withstand high pressures that build-up when the solid propellant burns inside (Fig. 2.7). The critical manufacturing processes adopted, included roll bending and L seam TIG welding of the maraging steel main section, ring rolling and stretching of bulkhead and age hardening.

▲   **Fig. 2.7**   *Solid Propellant Rocket Motor Static Testing*

(c) Machining of Magnesium Wings for *Prithvi*

The aerofoil wings used in the *Prithvi* missile have complex contours. To reduce the weight of the structure, the wings have been split into halves. Each half has a 3-D profile on one side and a complex, ribbed structure on the rear with a number of pockets. To make the wings light, the material in the rear surface is scooped out to the maximum possible extent. The Numerically Controlled (NC) tool path is programmed such that the ribbed structure is formed by the uncut material. The outer surface is supported by ribs at the back, designed to withstand aerodynamic loads. As the material in the pockets is scooped out, the bottom surface of the pockets emerge as 3-D surfaces parallel to the outer surface. The entire process has been completed using Computer Aided Design (CAD) and Computer Aided Manufacturing (CAM) facilities. The model for analysis was used to generate NC data and the tool path simulation for error-free NC programs. The technologies for fabrication were established and transferred to Hindustan Aeronautics Limited, Bangalore for production along with the manufacture of the 4-axis CNC profiler. The same ribs are used for drilling and rivetting purposes.

(d) Manufacture of *Vikas* Engine for PSLV

A significant development in aerospace manufacturing technology was the second stage of a PSLV, comprising of the *Vikas* engine based on liquid propulsion. This turbo-pump fed engine produces about 74 tonnes of thrust. The engine has three principal components—the gas generator, the turbo-pump, and the combustion chamber. It uses Unsymmetrical Di-Methyl Hydrazine (UDMH) as fuel and nitrogen tetroxide as oxidiser. The propellants are hypergolic, i.e., they ignite simultaneously when brought into contact with each other. A small quantity of propellants is burnt in the gas generator and the hot gases are cooled to 600 °C by spraying water. These hot gases and steam then pass to the turbo pump which drives the turbine. The rotating turbine turns two pumps, one for each of the propellants. These pumps feed about 250 kg of propellant under high pressure, which is injected into a thrust chamber and thereafter expelled through a nozzle. Making the *Vikas* engine involved high-precision fabrication. The critical manufacturing processes adopted for manufacturing the engine include stretch forming of cones for 3-D profile of thrust chamber assembly, 4/5-axis machining of impellers, shrink fitting of AI and SS material, and critical spline cutting of impellers.

(e) *Kaveri* Combuster

Combuster design technology is quite complex and requires a thorough understanding of the combustion phenomena, which includes fuel spray droplet dynamics, airflow patterns, and chemical kinetics. The design and development of annular combusters have been preferred to those of the can-type or can-annular type. Efforts in designing and developing are supplemented by experimental studies such as water flow visualisation, wire frame modelling, shape optimisation, and combuster model tests.

State-of-the-art technology has been developed for producing an optimum atomiser configuration for gas turbine combusters. The atomisers so developed also meet the stringent military specifications. Specialised techniques have also been employed for the fabrication of the combuster and its components in Perspex materials to aid flow visualisation. Reduction of the weight was one of the main aspects of the combuster design improvements. Accordingly, refinements in the design were carried out in certain areas of the combuster during development without sacrificing the performance requirements.

(f) Air Bottles

Superplasticity is the ability of certain materials to undergo extraordinary tensile deformation (usually more than 300%) without fracturing. Superplastic forming offers many advantages, including the elimination of unnecessary joints.

Titanium alloy air bottles have been developed through superplastic forming and electron beam welding. The superplastic forming route was developed by Defence Metallurgical Research Laboratory (DMRL) and the technology has been transferred to Mishra Dhatu Nigam Ltd.

(MIDHANI), Hyderabad. Figure 2.8 depicts the current manufacturing processes.

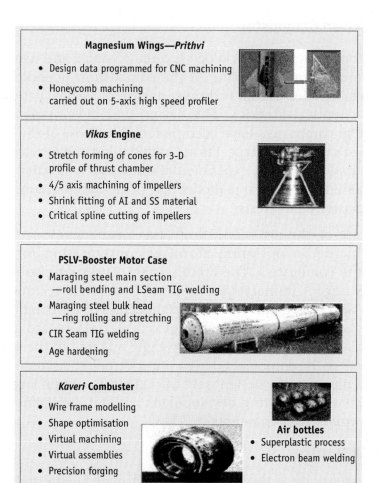

▲   **Fig. 2.8**   *Present Manufacturing Processes*

(g) Onboard Computer for Flight Systems

An onboard computer for a launch vehicle/missile system has to be loaded with the flight trajectory, the mission profile

(Fig. 2.9) and housekeeping operations of the launch vehicle/ missile. The flight software is also embedded in the onboard computer. For a given time and speed of a flight, including the error characteristics during the flight duration, the computer decides what, when and how much corrective control forces should be taken in real-time as a quick response, if an error builds up in the flight direction.

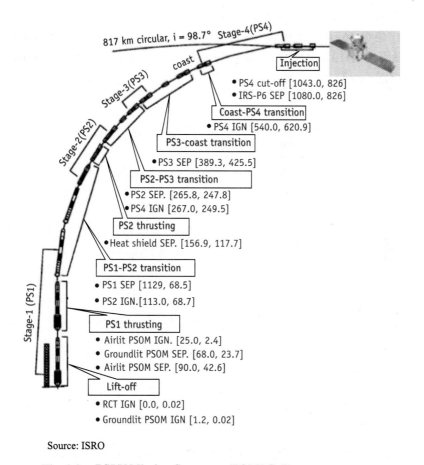

817 km circular, i = 98.7° Stage-4(PS4)

coast

Stage-3(PS3)

Stage-2(PS2)

Injection

- PS4 cut-off [1043.0, 826]
- IRS-P6 SEP [1080.0, 826]

Coast-PS4 transition
- PS4 IGN [540.0, 620.9]

PS3-coast transition
- PS3 SEP [389.3, 425.5]

PS2-PS3 transition
- PS2 SEP. [265.8, 247.8]
- PS4 IGN [267.0, 249.5]

PS2 thrusting
- Heat shield SEP. [156.9, 117.7]

PS1-PS2 transition
- PS1 SEP [1129, 68.5]
- PS2 IGN.[113.0, 68.7]

PS1 thrusting
- Airlit PSOM IGN. [25.0, 2.4]
- Groundlit PSOM SEP. [68.0, 23.7]
- Airlit PSOM SEP. [90.0, 42.6]

Lift-off
- RCT IGN [0.0, 0.02]
- Groundlit PSOM IGN [1.2, 0.02]

Stage-1 (PS1)

Source: ISRO

▲ **Fig. 2.9 *PSLV Mission Sequence (PSLV C–5)***

This involves right choices of VLSI devices, transistors, electronic relays, and conventional passive devices like capacitors and resistors. The onboard avionics architecture is designed and built with sub-systems like an inertial navigation system, an onboard computer, pulse code modulation telemetry, and missile interface units connected with the launch control centre.

Yet another design requirement for onboard computers is the capacity to withstand EMI effect for MIL standards. This onboard computer is digitally simulated for its performance, taking into account various failure modes. The output from this simulation becomes the design input for the development of onboard computers.

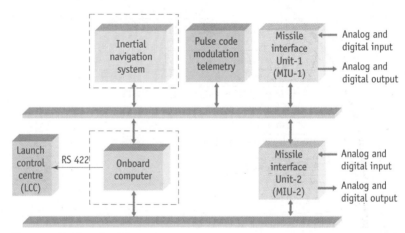

Features : Distributed architecture
Functions: OBC check-out, Pre-launch and auto-launch guidance, control and mission sequencing
INS   : Levelling and navigation
MIU   : Data acquisition, control command generation, power M-off, pyro firing

▲ **Fig. 2.10** *Typical Onboard Avionics Architecture*

After development, the onboard computer goes through a hardware in loop simulation. The computer, with its other guidance systems such as gyros and signal processing sub-systems, is connected to a digital ground computer and a simulator simulating all the three axes of flight pitch, yaw and roll. Again the failure modes are injected into the software and hardware with wind conditions to test the design robustness and verifying performance. Figure 2.10 depicts the onboard avionics architecture.

DESIGN INTEGRATED MANUFACTURING

We have made a leap from CAM to design integrated manufacturing for aerospace systems and automobiles. Virtual Reality (VR) simulations have also evolved. The additional feature now is a new software that provides immersive visualisation of a 3D environment. This technology has been used for walk-throughs in LCA prototypes which is saving 40% of the design time in the LCA undercarriage assembly and environmental control system bay. Similar VR models have been used in designing Indica car of Tata Engineering. Figure 2.11 represents design integrated manufacturing—virtual reality.

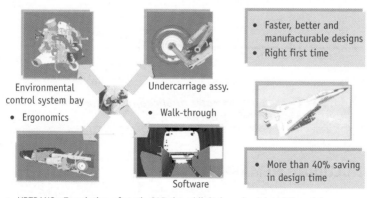

- VRTRANS : Translation of static CAD data (digital mockup) into VR model
- PRANA : Add life to VR model ⟶ virtual prototype

▲ **Fig. 2.11** *Design Integrated Manufacturing—Virtual Reality*

Figure 2.12 represents a review of advancement in design integrated manufacturing methodologies in the last few decades from numeric control to virtual reality mode design and simulation and flexible automated robotic computer integrated manufacturing.

In the 21st century, we see that all the functions such as design, drafting, manufacturing drawing, process planning, methods engineering, materials handling and manufacturing and inspection have been totally integrated, improving quality and precision resulting in lower rejection rate and faster cycle time from design to market.

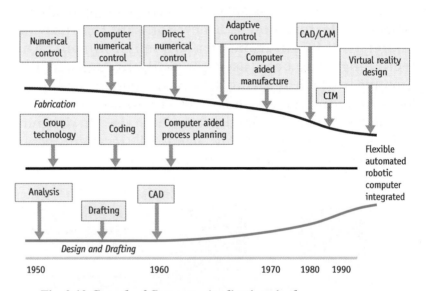

Fig. 2.12 *Growth of Computer Applications in the Manufacturing Sector*

CONCLUDING REMARKS

The success of the space programme through the launch of PSLV and GSLV missions, the successful development of missiles under the IGMDP and the recent test flights of LCA, strategic progress in nuclear energy programme prove that the Indian industries have the necessary manufacturing strength to undertake projects of national importance. This can further be augmented by adoption of indigenously developed state-of-the-art manufacturing processes.

Our vision for the Indian industry encompasses not only assembly and fabrication but also entire design capability and the capacity to cost-effective manufacturing with quality. To achieve an industrial leadership position, it is vital to acquire design capability and technology. This is possible with strategic partnership of R&D laboratories, academia and industry. Above all, management leadership to lead diverse industries in a particular area is critical. Technology is a valuable asset from research to marketing of a product. The result of this has been seen in the First Green Revolution in Agriculture. We will now discuss the impact of value addition in the Agriculture.

3

Value Addition in Agriculture

INTRODUCTION

This chapter covers the need for food and nutritional security, and the employment potential in the agriculture sector. Technologies that will result in higher productivity at various phases of seed-to-grain, seed-to-vegetable, seed-to-fruit, and milk production are discussed here.

This chapter focuses on the Second Green Revolution, comparing it in terms of technologies to the First Green Revolution. It also presents the thoughts of some visionaries about agriculture.

*Dr. Kalam interacting with farmers of Bihar at Sangrampur (RP Channel 5
Distributory) and appreciating the higher paddy and wheat production*

> **"** First Green Revolution transformed India to self-reliance from *'ship to mouth'** situation; the Second Green Revolution will ship food grains and products to many nations **"**

STRATEGY FOR AGRICULTURE

Foodgrains and products provide national security and agriculture products enhance geo-political and geo-commercial value.

As part of the First Green Revolution, India has reached self-sufficiency in food by producing 200 million tonnes (MT)

First Green Revolution

| Seed |
| Fertilisers |
| Water management |
| Training farmers |
| Cultivation management |
| Harvest and post harvest |
| Output = Grain (200 million tonnes) |

Green revolution 1970

Second Green Revolution

| Soil characterisation |
| Matching the seed |
| Fertiliser management |
| Water management |
| Training |
| Cultivation |
| Post-harvesting (SILOS) |
| Food processing (value addition) |
| Marketing |

▲   **Fig. 3.1   *The Green Revolutions***

Ship to mouth: During the food shortage in the 1960's, India was awaiting wheat-laden ships (PL480) to bring food.

of various varieties of food materials like cereals, vegetables and fruit (Fig. 3.1). Over a period of time there has been a gradual increase in the input cost of agriculture. The increase in agricultural output has not resulted in a proportionate increase in overall agriculture income. In addition, the scope for bringing more land under cultivation has reduced. Government and farmers have to face these problems and work for increasing productivity. India should have a mission to achieve a minimum production of 360 million MT of food grains in the next two decades. This will provide for domestic consumption, leave a sufficient margin for exports and also in the aid of other countries.

As employment in agriculture reduces to 60%, with a doubling in the demand for food, measures like deploying higher-level research, technology, agricultural extension services, and training will need to be instituted. Figure 3.2

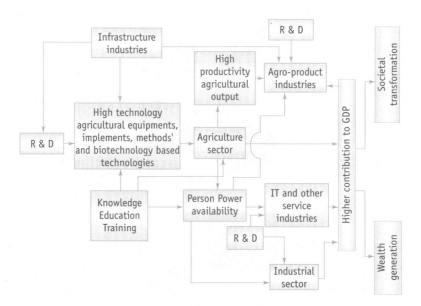

▲ **Fig. 3.2** *Strategy for Employment Generation*

explains that R&D, infrastructure industries, education and training can lead to augmentation in agriculture sector in the form of high technology agricultural equipment, biotechnology based technologies and complementary methods. Augmentation in this sector will lead to high agricultural productivity and free agricultural personnel for other sectors like IT & Services, industrial sector and agro-product industries. The net result will be a higher contribution to GDP.

BIODIVERSITY–TECHNOLOGY–PROSPERITY MATRIX

One of the core competencies of India is biodiversity, which combined with technology, will yield value-added products. Other countries which are rich in biodiversity include China, Brazil, Indonesia, Mexico, and Malaysia.

While on the other end of the spectrum we have technologically advanced nations like USA, Japan, France, Germany, and UK, which are not rich in biodiversity. There are also some regions in the deserts of Africa and Asia which are poor in both biodiversity and technology. This situation is represented in Fig. 3.3 and depicts that no nation has both of these competencies.

To tap the immense power of biodiversity, technology is needed for developing a genetically engineered seed or transforming a molecule extracted from a herb into a drug. What is needed is the integration of productivity in agriculture, biodiversity and technology.

India has to graduate to the fourth quadrant where both biodiversity and technology are in their prime. This situation will lead to value addition in agriculture, herbal and medicinal products.

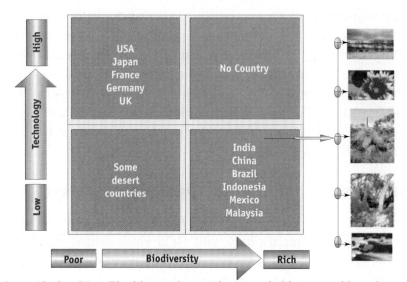

Source: Khoshoo T.N. – 'Bio rich countries must become tech-rich to reap ultimate harvest approaches to compensation, vol. 12, no. 3, 1996.'

▲   **Fig. 3.3   *Biodiversity–Technology–Prosperity Matrix***

AGRICULTURE AND FOOD PROCESSING

TIFAC had formed a national team to evolve a vision for transforming the nation from a developing country into a developed one by the year 2020. One of the key thrust areas was agriculture and food processing. A technology vision panel of TIFAC on agriculture and food processing has provided very important recommendations.

In the production of cereals, milk, rice, fruit and vegetables, India now occupies the first three positions in the world, while in productivity we rank 50th.

India's food requirement from the agricultural and agro-food sectors with the existing levels of production in cereal, milk, fruit and vegetables, have been studied along with the technologies needed. Here we discuss the possibilities of higher production in the next 20 years.

Agro-food: Cereals

With a base food production of 200 MT, expert analyses indicate that the business created by this production has a value of Rs 90,000 crore per year and the related industries contribute another Rs 9,000 crore per year, particularly in packaging and value-addition. The losses due to poor preservation, storage, and rodent problems cost Rs 9,000 crore per year.

The panel has recommended certain core technologies such as pest/rodent control, SILO-based storage, packaging, handling equipment, automatic weighing, and electronic sensors (for moisture, etc.) that will result in high productivity. These measures and the addition of core technologies would lead to a production volume of 360 MT by 2020. The business would then be doubled to Rs 150,000 crore per year while other related business like packaging and value addition would touch about Rs 90,000 crore and losses would be substantially reduced to about Rs 3,000 crore per year (Fig. 3.4). Indeed this is a great mission for the technologists working with farmers and consumers.

Agro-Food: Milk, Fruit, and Vegetables

Similar recommendations for fruit, vegetables and milk by the expert committees for higher productivity and core technology deployment are provided in Fig. 3.4.

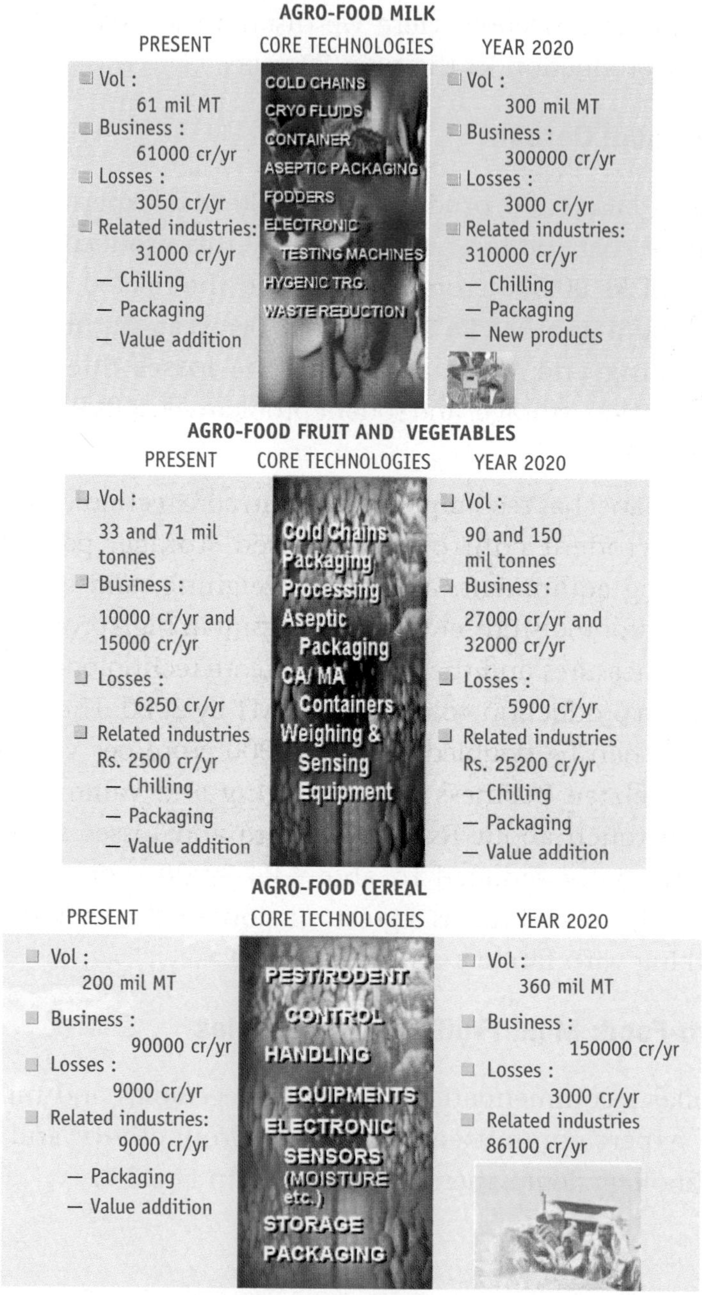

AGRO-FOOD MILK

PRESENT	CORE TECHNOLOGIES	YEAR 2020
Vol :	COLD CHAINS	Vol :
61 mil MT	CRYO FLUIDS	300 mil MT
Business :	CONTAINER	Business :
61000 cr/yr	ASEPTIC PACKAGING	300000 cr/yr
Losses :	FODDERS	Losses :
3050 cr/yr	ELECTRONIC	3000 cr/yr
Related industries:	TESTING MACHINES	Related industries:
31000 cr/yr	HYGENIC TRG.	310000 cr/yr
— Chilling	WASTE REDUCTION	— Chilling
— Packaging		— Packaging
— Value addition		— New products

AGRO-FOOD FRUIT AND VEGETABLES

PRESENT	CORE TECHNOLOGIES	YEAR 2020
Vol :	Cold Chains	Vol :
33 and 71 mil tonnes	Packaging	90 and 150 mil tonnes
Business :	Processing	Business :
10000 cr/yr and 15000 cr/yr	Aseptic Packaging	27000 cr/yr and 32000 cr/yr
Losses :	CA/ MA	Losses :
6250 cr/yr	Containers	5900 cr/yr
Related industries Rs. 2500 cr/yr	Weighing & Sensing Equipment	Related industries Rs. 25200 cr/yr
— Chilling		— Chilling
— Packaging		— Packaging
— Value addition		— Value addition

AGRO-FOOD CEREAL

PRESENT	CORE TECHNOLOGIES	YEAR 2020
Vol :	PESTIRODENT	Vol :
200 mil MT	CONTROL	360 mil MT
Business :	HANDLING	Business :
90000 cr/yr	EQUIPMENTS	150000 cr/yr
Losses :	ELECTRONIC	Losses :
9000 cr/yr	SENSORS	3000 cr/yr
Related industries:	(MOISTURE etc.)	Related industries
9000 cr/yr	STORAGE	86100 cr/yr
— Packaging	PACKAGING	
— Value addition		

▲ **Fig. 3.4   *Agro-Food: Scenario 2020***

TECHNOLOGY FOR COLD DESERT
CULTIVATION: A CASE STUDY

A collaborative experiment in the 4000 m high valley of Jammu & Kashmir (Nang village in Ladakh) by the field research laboratory of the Defence Research and Development Organisation (DRDO) and the Indian Council of Agricultural Research (ICAR) used the villagers' efforts for the mission of round the year cultivation. Integrated activities of water harvesting in three reservoirs, afforestation of 25 hectares wasteland, potato seed production for Leh valley, greenhouse cultivation, and improved agro-technology and machinery have been implemented. Figures 3.5 and 3.6 show the various actions taken for afforestation and agriculture in the hilly region.

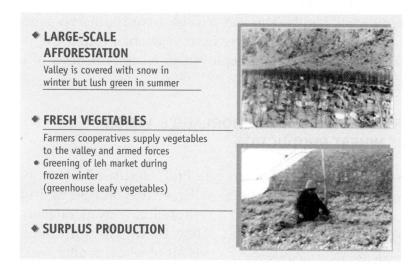

◆ **LARGE-SCALE AFFORESTATION**

Valley is covered with snow in winter but lush green in summer

◆ **FRESH VEGETABLES**

Farmers cooperatives supply vegetables to the valley and armed forces
• Greening of leh market during frozen winter (greenhouse leafy vegetables)

◆ **SURPLUS PRODUCTION**

▲ **Fig. 3.5**   *Greening of the Leh Valley*

NANG (4000 m) LADAKH, JAMMU & KASHMIR

Field research laboratory (Defence
Research and Development Organisation)
and Indian Council of Agricultural Research
as partners used village cooperative efforts

◈ **Activities Undertaken**

- ✓ Water harvesting (three reservoirs)
- ✓ Afforestation in 25 hectare wasteland
- ✓ Potato seed production for Leh valley
- ✓ Greenhouse cultivation
- ✓ Improved agro-technology and machinery

▲ **Fig. 3.6   *Cold Desert: Self Sustaining Village***

As a result of the above integrated actions, within two years the farmers increased their annual income from Rs 2200 to Rs 4400 per family. This was possible as the farmers organised a cooperative for supplying fresh vegetables round the year. This experience can be deployed in all hilly regions of our country.

PROFESSOR NORMAN BORLAUG'S VISION OF WHEAT PRODUCTION

Sometime back, Nobel laureate Prof. Norman Borlaug, who was associated with the First Green Revolution of India,

> *Biotechnology will also assist in developing pest-resistant seeds that would lead to a 10% increase in the productivity.*

lectured at Vigyan Bhavan in New Delhi. He unfurled the vision of wheat production for the world population for the next two decades. Today, the world's population is 6 billion. In 20 years, it will increase to 8 billion people. To support this growing number, food production has to double—but within the same available area and water or even lesser. Only technology and efficient management can help in doubling the food production by improving existing agricultural practices and appropriately harnessing water and fertilisers, both inorganic and organic. Biotechnology will also assist in developing pest-resistant seeds that would lead to a 10% increase in the productivity.

SECOND GREEN REVOLUTION

The key concepts of this proposed Second Green Revolution (Fig. 3.1) are soil characterisation to suit the seeds, developing hybrid seeds and appropriate seed selection, suitable fertilisers, water management, farmer training, crop management, post harvest management, food processing and marketing. Success in this mission can be achieved through collaborative efforts of research scientists, water management authorities and most importantly farmers by being open to innovations and receptive to advance technology and training in all the areas of concern.

HIGHER YIELD OF AGRICULTURAL PRODUCTION AND TECHNOLOGY

To put the vision into action, the government had provided funds in the budget of 2000 for experimental development tasks in agriculture, higher education, industrial fields, multiple rural connectivity, power and advanced areas. We would like to share some experiences and results in specific areas. These are built on our earlier experiences with missions in the areas of sugar, fly ash, and composites.

Bihar Project

Late Prof. S K Sinha, a renowned agricultural scientist, the former Director of Indian Agriculture Research Institute and

TIFAC took up a project on *A System's Approach to Enhance Agricultural Productivity in Central Bihar and Eastern India*. The ICAR unit at Patna participated, and six villages of *RP* Channel 5 and 9 villages of Majhauli distributories were selected during the *kharif* season of 1998. The system's approach consisted of soil analysis, seed choice, cultivation season, fertiliser selection, and training to the farmers (particularly in the usage of remote sensing data).

This intensive collaboration of scientists and farmers resulted in increasing wheat production by nearly five tonnes/hectare (Figs 3.7 & 3.8). This effort is spreading fast to other areas and now nearly 200 villages are participating in the programme. We visited a few villages where this system's approach is being used, and found that the farmers are happy that both the production and their income have increased. Naturally, this ushers in equipment for faster harvesting, storage, and marketing as well as banking systems. We are glad that they have come up with ideas for problems and are also preparing to work together and share facilities.

Crop	No. of Distributories Covered		No. of Villages Covered		Area Covered (ha)		Yield		
	1999	2000	1999	2000	1999	2000	Traditional yield (t/ha)	1999 Demonstration yield (t/ha)	2000 Demonstration yield (t/ha)
Paddy	2	−	5	178	40	432	1.4	5.8	5.9
Wheat	2	−	11	200	16	∼ 1000	1.5	4.5	5.0

Fig. 3.7 *Results of the Total Systems Approach Technology*

Fig. 3.8 *Paddy Crop Ready to Harvest at Village Sangrampur (RP Channel 5 Distributory)*

There has been another very successful project of applying remote sensing to environmentally degraded land in certain parts of Uttar Pradesh. The area chosen contains high-intensity sodic land in the major canal commands—Upper Ganga, Lower Ganga, Ram Ganga, and Sharda Sahayak. Sodic land intensity is high in the critical and semi-critical waterlogged areas and partly in the areas that are likely to

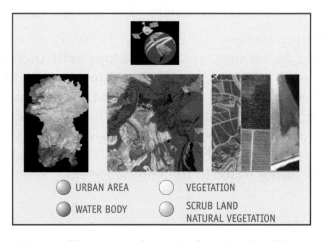

Fig. 3.9 *Satellite Imaging for Agriculture Land and Water*

get waterlogged. The Uttar Pradesh Remote Sensing Department, along with some other departments in Uttar Pradesh, studied the area under a World Bank funded project (Fig. 3.9). There has been tremendous success in reclaiming sodic land. Remote sensing is also being used for subsequent study of the successes and failures of reclamation measures. One of the studies indicates that the status of sodic land reclamation is variable in different hydrogeological conditions. Such lessons, derived from the project, are useful for enhancing the reclamation efforts.

CONCLUDING REMARKS

India's economic growth still largely depends on agriculture. Modern technologies integrated with agriculture and agro-food industry will revolutionise this sector and produce large scale employment and thereby wealth. It is said that "When users, implementers as well as knowledge and skill possessors are linked and networked, success comes effectively and in multiples". A network resource can impart a non-linear progressive addition to development and growth.

The introduction of the Second Green Revolution with training to farmers and technology will increase the agriculture production to 360 million tonnes by 2020. Improved storage and distribution and reduced wastage by post harvest management strategy will enable every citizen to get food, eliminating poverty. We are sure the young are ready to take up the challenge. Let us analyse the manufacturing sector in the knowledge era.

Manufacturing in the Knowledge Era

4

INTRODUCTION

This chapter brings out the progress made in the manufacturing field in light of the recent strides made with the advent of information and communication technology. Computer Aided Design (CAD) and Computer Aided Manufacturing (CAM) have revolutionised manufacturing and have led to rapid prototyping technologies and customised manufacturing. State-of-the-art techniques are increasingly in use like Automatic Materials Handling Systems (AMH), Automated Guided Vehicles, industrial robots, Flexible Manufacturing System (FMS), etc. Finally, the industrial scenario in India, with a special emphasis of the vital role played by small-scale industries has been highlighted.

Dr. Kalam with engineers and technicians in a manufacturing unit

ADVANCES IN MANUFACTURING AND MICRO-ELECTRONICS

Humanity has seen a rapid transformation in manufacturing in the last 150 years because of the advent of electricity and other new techniques. This revolution continued with the introduction of numerically controlled robotics. Lately, we are witnessing new trends, with the introduction of software and design tools. Though India was behind with respect to industrially advanced countries, now the time has come to utilise its core competence in software, design and

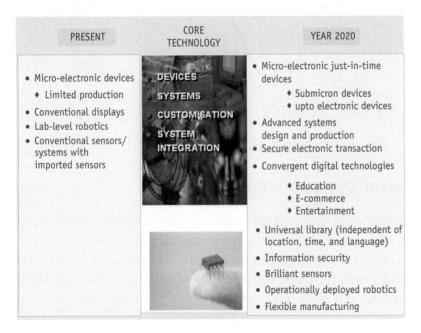

PRESENT	CORE TECHNOLOGY	YEAR 2020

• Micro-electronic devices
  ♦ Limited production
• Conventional displays
• Lab-level robotics
• Conventional sensors/
  systems with
  imported sensors
	DEVICES
	
	SYSTEMS
	
	CUSTOMISATION
	
	SYSTEM
	INTEGRATION
		• Micro-electronic just-in-time devices
		  ♦ Submicron devices
		  ♦ upto electronic devices
		• Advanced systems design and production
		• Secure electronic transaction
		• Convergent digital technologies
		  ♦ Education
		  ♦ E-commerce
		  ♦ Entertainment
		• Universal library (independent of location, time, and language)
		• Information security
		• Brilliant sensors
		• Operationally deployed robotics
		• Flexible manufacturing

▲ **Fig. 4.1** *Electronics and Sensors Manufacturing*

application of virtual reality. The year 2020 will witness considerable progress in convergent digital technologies, intelligent systems, microrobots and nanoelectronic systems, as applied to manufacturing (Fig. 4.1).

During the last six decade the progress in micro-electronics has been phenomenal, and this has added a new dimension to manufacturing. Figure 4.2 explains the progress from microprocessor in 1970s, to MEMS in 2000, and to nanotechnology. The future belongs to nanofabrication, bio-computing, molecular computing and quantum computing.

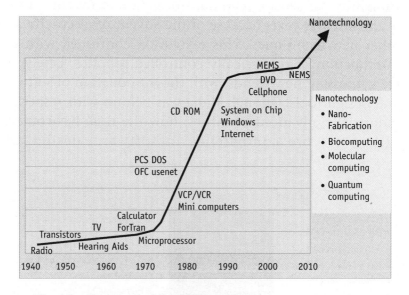

▲ **Fig. 4.2** *Progress in Micro-Electronics*

SMART SYSTEMS TECHNOLOGY

In the development of sensors, Micro-Electro Mechanical Systems (MEMS) technology has had a profound impact particularly with the miniaturisation of electronics. Miniaturisation not only reduces the size of the functional systems but also has a great potential to decrease the costs while at the same time increasing the speed, performance, reliability, capability and upgradability (Fig. 4.3). A further advancement is the development of nanotechnologies which is leading to miniaturisation and the development of highly efficient systems.

Nanotechnology involves manufacturing products by rearranging atoms and the properties of the product depend on how those atoms are arranged. When a nano particle or fibre is made it has a minimum surface/core defects due to its size and this increases its strength and modulus.

In the field of structural materials, nano particles have played an important role. When these particles are reinforced in polymetric matrix they increase mechanical properties manifold. The nanotubes are 100 times stronger and 60 times lighter than steel. Nanotubes find use in a variety of sensors for electronic applications and the development of nano scale machines. An academic institution in India has developed nanoelectronic junctions. R&D is under progress to develop Nano Electro-Mechanical Systems (NEMS) to replace MEMS for higher efficiencies and compactness.

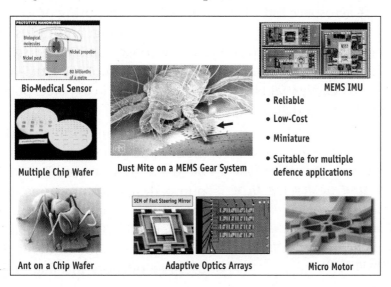

Fig. 4.3 *Micro-Electro Machanical Systems (MEMS)*

COMPUTER INTEGRATED MANUFACTURING

On account of advances in computing power (both hardware and software) it is now no longer necessary to make prototypes in a factory or a laboratory to study a new product. Many new products can be designed on computers and their behaviour simulated in the system.

By choosing an optimum design through such simulations, computer programs can directly drive the manufacturing processes. These processes are generally called Computer-Aided Design (CAD) and Computer-Aided Manufacturing (CAM).

These capabilities are leading to newer forms of demands by customers. Each customer can be offered several special options. Customised product design and flexible manufacturing are other popular techniques currently in vogue in many developed countries.

The tools used in manufacturing today have immensely multiplied: lasers and water jets are increasingly being used. In the aerospace industry, advanced manufacturing processes like friction stir welding, microwave welding, and diffusion bonding have been introduced. No longer, specialised steels or even ceramics monopolise the cutting tool industry. It is hard to believe that lasers can be used to cut heavy steel plates and also for a delicate eye surgery.

If we also, as a country and as a people, focus our efforts to eradicate poverty and to develop in a sustained manner, no obstacle would be able to withstand the force of that collective, coherent, and focused will!

Can you imagine that the plain water you use at home can be used to cut steel? Water pumped at high pressures and focused as a jet cuts through steel cleanly. This technology holds promise for underwater use, like offshore installations.

Anything focused, and focused sharply, becomes a good cutting tool or a welding source. A laser is a focused and coherent source of light. A water jet is a sharply directed high pressure jet. If we also, as a country and as a people, focus our efforts to eradicate poverty and to develop in a sustained manner, no obstacle would be able to withstand the force of that collective, coherent, and focused will!

India stands to gain enormously by the coupling of computers and the manufacturing process. We have many success stories, though small compared to the potential, which encourage us to share this vision.

Rapid prototyping technologies (or free form fabrication) can build up complex 3-D parts direct from CAD input without any other machinery (Fig. 4.4).

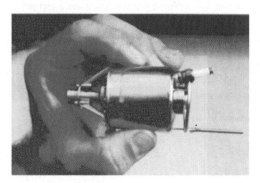

Miniature engine

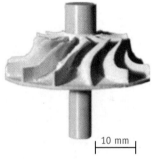

10 mm

Propeller made by rapid prototyping

▲ **Fig. 4.4** *Rapid Prototyping*

MANUFACTURING SECTOR

The Indian manufacturing sector can be broadly classified into two major categories:

1. Small-scale industries

2. Medium and large-scale industries

Small-Scale Industries

The small-scale industries (SSI) plays a vital role in the growth of the country and contributes almost 40% of the gross industrial value to the Indian economy.

It has been estimated that an investment of 1 million rupees in fixed assets in the SSI sector produces 4.62 million rupees worth of goods or services with tremendous value addition.

Over the years, the SSI sector has grown rapidly with impressive growth rates during the various Plan periods. The number of small-scale units has substantially increased from an estimated 0.87 million in 1980-81 to over 3 million in 2000.

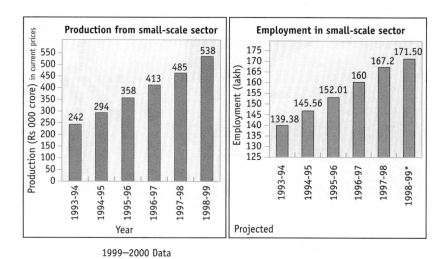

1999–2000 Data

Export	:	54,000 crore
No. of Units	:	32 lakh
No. of Sick Units	:	Less than 10%

▲ **Fig. 4.5** *Growth Profile of Small-Scale Industries*

The SSI sector in India creates the largest employment opportunity for the Indian populace, next only to agriculture. It plays a major role in India's present export performance contributing about 45%–50% of Indian exports. The direct exports from the SSI sector account for nearly 35% of the total exports. Besides direct exports, it is estimated that small-scale industrial units contribute around 15% to exports indirectly. This takes place through merchant exporters, trading houses, and export houses. They may also be in the form of export orders from large units or the production of parts and components for use in finished exportable goods. It would surprise many to know that non-traditional products account for more than 95% of SSI exports.

The product groups where the SSI sector dominates in exports are sports goods, readymade garments, woollen garments and knitwear, plastic products, processed food and leather products. The SSI sector is re-orienting its export strategy towards the new trade regime being ushered in by the World Trade Organisation (WTO).

Opportunities in Small-Scale Industries In a period of five years the employment potential in the SSI sector has increased from 140 lakh to 170 lakh. Growth profile of SSI is given in Fig. 4.5. The SSI sector has tremendous potential for the following reasons:

- Less capital-intensive
- Extensive promotion and support by government
- Funding: finance and subsidies
- Reservation for exclusive purchase by government
- Export promotion

The SSI sector has performed exceedingly well and enabled India to achieve a wide measure of industrial growth and diversification. This sector is ideally suited to build on the strengths of our traditional skills and knowledge, by infusion of technologies, capital, and innovative marketing practices. This is an opportune time to set up projects in the small-scale sector.

It may be said that the outlook is positive, indeed promising, given some safeguards. This expectation is based on an essential feature of the Indian industry and the demand structures. The diversity in production systems and demand structures will ensure long-term co-existence of many layers of demand for consumer products/technologies/processes. There will be flourishing and well-grounded markets for the same product/process, differentiated by quality, value addition, and sophistication. This characteristic of the Indian economy will allow complementary existence for diverse units. The promotional and protective policies of the

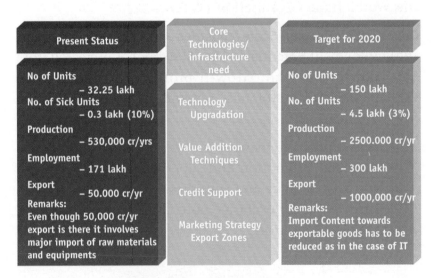

Present Status	Core Technologies/ infrastructure need	Target for 2020
No of Units – 32.25 lakh No. of Sick Units – 0.3 lakh (10%) Production – 530,000 cr/yrs Employment – 171 lakh Export – 50.000 cr/yr Remarks: Even though 50,000 cr/yr export is there it involves major import of raw materials and equipments	Technology Upgradation Value Addition Techniques Credit Support Marketing Strategy Export Zones	No of Units – 150 lakh No. of Units – 4.5 lakh (3%) Production – 2500.000 cr/yr Employment – 300 lakh Export – 1000,000 cr/yr Remarks: Import Content towards exportable goods has to be reduced as in the case of IT

Fig. 4.6 *Potential in Small-Scale Industries*

government have ensured the presence of this sector in an astonishing range of products, particularly consumer goods. However, the deficiencies of the sector have been the inadequacies in capital, technology upgradation, and marketing. The process of liberalisation will, therefore, attract the infusion of exactly these ingradients into the sector. Figure 4.6 indicates the potential in Small Scale Industries.

Medium and Large Industries

Today industries mostly depend on licensing technologies; which is why we are not in a position to enjoy the benefits of industrialisation as expected. To overcome this situation, Indian industries should form consortiums with R&D laboratories and work together to develop their own technologies and become exporters of technology products.

One relevant experience is the formation of Non-Ferrous Materials Technology Development Centre (NFTDC) integrating large-scale industries in a production establishment for low-volume, high-cost products, bringing together multiple technologies developed in their R&D laboratories. The management is decentralised, with a focus on R&D.

In the pursuit of all-round economic growth, the physical and social well-being of all our people, and national security, we may have to ensure the creation of an enabling environment to try something uniquely Indian.

Such an inventive spirit will be useful for the long-term sustainability of our gains.

While there are a number of strengths in this area, there are also several technological weaknesses. For example, we depend upon imported machinery for quality production. The TIFAC Task Force teams, which have looked at these aspects in totality, are confident that India can be a leading textile producing country and become a top player in the global market (Fig. 4.7).

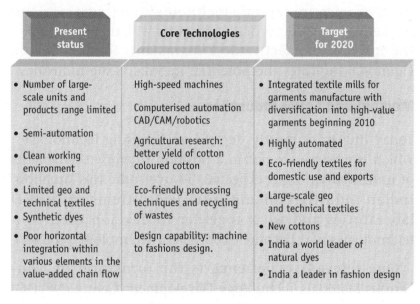

Present status	Core Technologies	Target for 2020
• Number of large-scale units and products range limited • Semi-automation • Clean working environment • Limited geo and technical textiles • Synthetic dyes • Poor horizontal integration within various elements in the value-added chain flow	High-speed machines Computerised automation CAD/CAM/robotics Agricultural research: better yield of cotton coloured cotton Eco-friendly processing techniques and recycling of wastes Design capability: machine to fashions design.	• Integrated textile mills for garments manufacture with diversification into high-value garments beginning 2010 • Highly automated • Eco-friendly textiles for domestic use and exports • Large-scale geo and technical textiles • New cottons • India a world leader of natural dyes • India a leader in fashion design

Fig. 4.7 *Vision 2020 for Textile Industry*

India is the third largest producer of coal and a global player too. The productivity in underground mining requires a quantum jump from 0.5 tonne per man-year in the immediate near term. In addition, we have to work on clean coal technology to prevent the effects of global warming and environmental pollution. For a long time we have been talking about integrated gasification and combined cycle technology. NTPC, BHEL and CSIR laboratories should help in this project by contributing in benefication and washing of the coal input. There should be a time bound programme for getting the results from this project. All mining operations today involve continuous use of explosives, thereby generating high noise level, vibrations and shocks and very high level of dust pollution. This also takes away very large area as explosive safety zone and environment safety zone. Our researchers must evolve a technology for using high power laser system for safe, pollution free and precision mining.

We should undertake technology upgradation, productivity improvement, energy conservation, environmental protection, and quality improvement. This will include use of CAD/CAM, robotics, high-speed machines, material handling systems, electronic instrumentation, and computerised automation.

Figure 4.8 attempts to capture these details in a simple form with the first part presenting highlights of the current status, the third part being the vision for 2020, and the second portion highlighting core technologies to be mastered. Figure 4.9 depicts the vision for Engineering Industries-II.

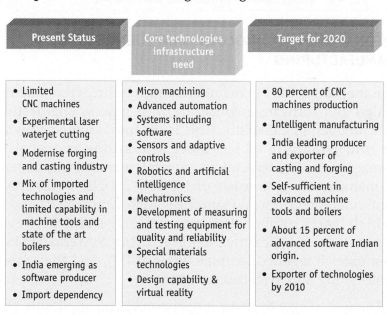

Present Status	Core technologies infrastructure need	Target for 2020
• Limited CNC machines • Experimental laser waterjet cutting • Modernise forging and casting industry • Mix of imported technologies and limited capability in machine tools and state of the art boilers • India emerging as software producer • Import dependency	• Micro machining • Advanced automation • Systems including software • Sensors and adaptive controls • Robotics and artificial intelligence • Mechatronics • Development of measuring and testing equipment for quality and reliability • Special materials technologies • Design capability & virtual reality	• 80 percent of CNC machines production • Intelligent manufacturing • India leading producer and exporter of casting and forging • Self-sufficient in advanced machine tools and boilers • About 15 percent of advanced software Indian origin. • Exporter of technologies by 2010

▲ **Fig. 4.8** *Vision 2020 for Engineering Industries-I*

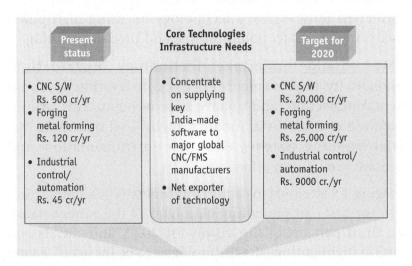

Fig. 4.9 *Vision 2020 for Engineering Industries-II*

INFORMATION TECHNOLOGY'S INFLUENCE IN MANUFACTURING

The application of IT in manufacturing has three components: design and software engineering with process engineering and production capability. This is, in turn, connected with an understanding of customer aspirations and quality management. The technology, which is a crucial component of manufacturing, consists of NC, CNC, DNC, CAD/CAM/ Computer Aided Process Planning (CAPP), Automated Guided Vehicle (AGV)/Robot/Automated Storage and Retrieval Systems (ASRS)/Flexible Manufacturing Systems (FMS)/ Computer Integrated Manufacturing (CIM), and then rapid prototyping and Web-based design.

The technology to make it operational and applicable and the methodology to be used are concurrent engineering, robust design, Group Technology (GT), Just in Time (JIT), Manufacturing Resource Planning (MRP-II), Enterprise Resource Planning (ERP). It can be seen that the application of IT in manufacturing integrates knowledge, skills, manufacturing, tools and techniques, and manpower (Fig. 4.10).

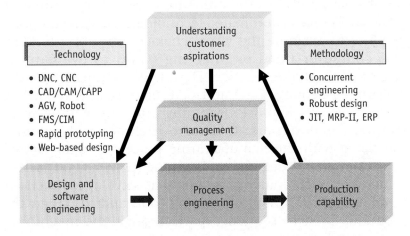

Knowledge, skills, infrastructure, tools and techniques, and manpower

Fig. 4.10 *Application of IT in Manufacturing*

MANUFACTURING IN THE STRATEGIC SECTOR

In the past few years, many advances have taken place in manufacturing in the strategic sector in India. Substantial progress has also been made in the areas of design and process engineering with increasing applications of computers. The advent of new technologies like CAD/CAM, FMS/CIM, Rapid Prototyping, Web-based design, and VR together with new and innovative management methodologies like concurrent engineering has enabled the production of high-quality defence products with reduced cost and time for product realisation. The process has been further accelerated with the advent of novel hardware systems in manufacturing like robotics and CNC machines. Over the years, state-of-the-art manufacturing technologies have been used by ISRO in its development programme for launch vehicles, by DRDO in its missile programmes, and by ADA in its LCA project all with notable success.

In the area of software, the CAD approach to product and process design utilises the immense power of the computer. CAD covers several automated technologies such as computer graphics to examine the visual characteristics of a product and computer-aided engineering (CAE) to evaluate its engineering characteristics. Design is no longer a time-consuming activity. CAD and CAE have been extended to techniques like Rapid Prototyping and VR, making work simpler for designers. CAD also includes technologies associated with the manufacturing process design, referred to as Computer-Aided Process Planning (CAPP). CAPP is used to design the computer programs that serve as instructions to computer-controlled machining tools and to design the programs used to sequence parts though the machining centres and other processes needed to complete the part. Sophisticated CAD systems are also able to do on-screen tests, replacing the early phases of prototype testing and modification. Automated Manufacturing, Planning, and Control Systems (MP&CS) are simply computer-based information systems that help plan, schedule, and monitor a manufacturing operation. They obtain information from the factory floor continuously about work status, material arrivals, so on and release production and purchase orders.

All these automated technologies are brought together under CIM. It is the automated version of the manufacturing process where the three major manufacturing functions—product and process design, planning and control, and the manufacturing process itself—are integrated by the automated technologies described above. Further, the traditional integration mechanism of oral and written communication is replaced by computer technology. Such highly automated and integrated manufacturing is also, called the 'Factory of the Future'. The Heavy Alloy Penetrator Plant (HAPP) in Tiruchirapalli is an example where this concept has been applied for manufacture of FSAPDS (Fin Stabilised Armour Piercing Discading Sabot). Established in 1988, this factory has led to tight tolerances consistency and repeatability in production, lower rejection rates, and large production volumes (Fig. 4.11). What would have normally required 600 workers is being carried out faster and to the required quality with an 80 member team.

Factory of the future

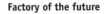

• Tight tolerances (stabilisation) • Consistency and replicability • Lower rejection rate	Fin stabilised armour piercing discarding sabot (FSAPDS)	• Large production volume • Multiple range • Stringent quality requirements

Fully automated facility established in 1988 for producing multiple types of FSAPDS

▲ **Fig. 4.11** *Heavy Alloy Penetrator Plant (HAPP)*

The hardware systems for manufacturing have become extremely advanced, especially with the advent of computers. The machining lathes of yesteryear are being phased out and replaced by advanced machinery. Machining is now carried out through FMS, machining centres and automatic materials handling systems. NC machines comprise a single machine tool and a computer that controls the sequence of processes performed on the machine. Machining centres represent increased levels of automation. They not only provide, automatic control of the machine, but also carry many tools that can be automatically changed depending on the operation. Further, materials handling on the shop-floor has been augmented with Automated Materials Handling (AMH) systems, which improve the efficiency of transportation, storage, and retrieval of materials. Examples are computerised conveyors and automatic storage and retrieval systems (ASRS) in which computers direct automatic loaders to pick and place items.

Automated Guided Vehicle (AGV) systems use embedded floor wires to direct driverless vehicles to various locations in the plant. AGVs with Infra Red (IR) sensors are being used for automatic obstacle avoidance. Besides, materials handling, industrial robots are being used as substitutes for workers for many repetitive manual activities and tasks that are dangerous, dirty, or simply dull. Robots also provide a faster, better, and cheaper way of doing work (Fig. 4.12). A robot is a programmable multifunctional machine that may be equipped with an end effector. Examples of end effectors include a gripper to pick things up or a tool such as a wrench, a welder, or a paint sprayer. Advanced capabilities have been designed into robots to allow vision, tactile sensing, and hand-to-hand coordination. In addition, some models can be taught a sequence of motions in a three-dimensional patterns. In the area of surgery, robo-surgery has ushered in a path breaking procedure, by employing robots for performing complex heart surgeries. Such procedures can entail the use of endoscopic cameras and arms fitted with robotic the fingers called 'endowrists' which are microscopic tools which can be directed to perform all the movements of a normal surgeon like cut, sew, swivel etc. This, besides enhancing patient safety, has been found to be less costlier than conventional surgery.

Individual parts of the automation can be combined to form a FMS, a totally automated machine system that consists of machine centres with automated loading and unloading of parts, an AGV system for transportation of parts between machine, and other automated elements.

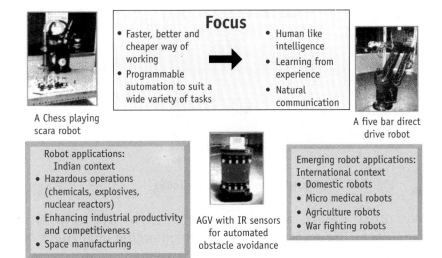

A Chess playing scara robot

Focus
- Faster, better and cheaper way of working
- Programmable automation to suit a wide variety of tasks

- Human like intelligence
- Learning from experience
- Natural communication

A five bar direct drive robot

Robot applications:
Indian context
- Hazardous operations (chemicals, explosives, nuclear reactors)
- Enhancing industrial productivity and competitiveness
- Space manufacturing

AGV with IR sensors for automated obstacle avoidance

Emerging robot applications:
International context
- Domestic robots
- Micro medical robots
- Agriculture robots
- War fighting robots

▲ **Fig. 4.12** *Some Applications of Robots*

All the CIM technologies are tied together using a network and integrated database. For instance, data integration allows CAD systems to be linked to CAM, while NC parts programme and the manufacturing planning and controlled systems can be linked to AMH systems to facilitate parts pick-up. Therefore, in a fully integrated system, the areas of design, testing, fabrication, assembly, inspection, and material handling are not only automated but also integrated with each other and with the manufacturing schedule functions.

PRODUCT VALUE ADDITION

Figure 4.13 shows the potential for value addition in a product per employee as a comparison of some countries. India has to work hard in value addition techniques in its manufacturing industries, in honing the core competency of skilled manpower, in procuring raw materials, and in upgrading capital equipment.

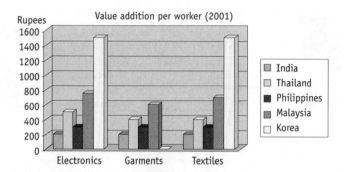

▲ **Fig. 4.13** *Value Addition Potential in India*

We must create a sound environment to help the manufacturing sector cope with the emerging challenges of globalisation. This could include the following measures.

- Special thrust on modernisation and technology upgradation of existing units
- Special package for promotion and development of small and village enterprises
- Consortium of Indian R&D laboratories and industries to gain design development that will enhance competitiveness
- Technology support
- Marketing support
- Credit support
- Entrepreneurship development
- Promotion of self-employment
- Infrastructure
- Facilitation

CONCLUDING REMARKS

We have discussed the SSI sector in detail, because of its great potential for rural development and employment provision. The large industries are the mother of small industries and help the national development functions.

For building a Developed India, apart from resources and human power, which we have in abundance, we need young leaders who can command the transformation. Leaders are the creators of new organisations of excellence. Quality leaders are like magnets who will attract the best people to build the team for the organisation and provide inspiring leadership even during adverse conditions. And they are not afraid of risks. Like the manufacturing sector, today we see revolution taking place in the healthcare sector.

Healthcare Revolution

INTRODUCTION

This chapter discusses the various mechanisms required for strengthening the healthcare sector in India, and ensuring 'Health for All' by the year 2020. The importance of technology driven healthcare systems and spin-offs from defence technologies have also been discussed. As India is rich in bio-diversity, traditional medicine and extraction of medicines from herbs have been presented. Moreover, the promising role of biotechnology for improving healthcare has been discussed. Measures to improve nutrition, healthcare facilities and hygiene awareness have been addressed.

- *How will healthcare delivery institutions be shaped in the future?*
- *What are the trends and transformations that await us in the coming years?*
- *How are we going to merge technology, management and medicine into a workable and economically feasible combination?*
- *What are the barriers that we shall certainly encounter, and how can we overcome them?*
- *And, what are the research questions that we should address?*

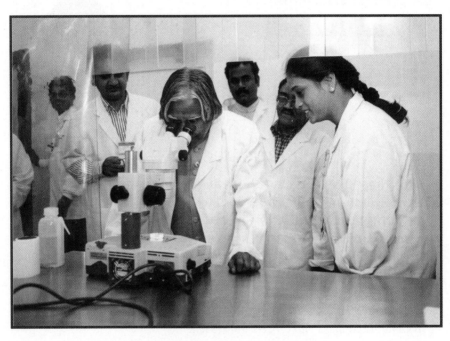

Dr. Kalam in a Biotechnology Lab

"Technologies must relieve the pain of society"

TECHNOLOGY VISION 2020 FOR HEALTHCARE

India is a vast country with diverse climatic conditions and a very large population. Due to inadequate healthcare facilities, lack of awareness about hygiene, and malnutrition, a wide spectrum of diseases occur.

Population and Healthcare

The outstanding developmental efforts mounted at various levels in the country during the last four decades have resulted in a very definite demographic transition in many states. The current single digit death-rate in some states is comparable

Comparison of India and the US

Population Details	India	US
Birth-rate	25–30	14.7
Death-rate	8	4.7
Population increase rate	17	10

(Unit: Numbers per 1000 per year)

Fig. 5.1 ***Population Increase Rate***

to many European countries and is getting stabilised at 8 per 1000 people per year. The current birth-rate is around 25–30 per thousand per year, and in Bihar, Uttar Pradesh and Madhya Pradesh it is higher than the rest of India, resulting in a national population increase of 17 per thousand per year (Fig. 5.1). It has been observed that in states with a high women's literacy, the birth-rate is controlled. Therefore, emphasis should be laid on women's education.

Healthcare Vision 2020

The Technology Vision 2020 for Healthcare was evolved by a panel of healthcare specialists drawn from various parts of the country. The team studied the core strengths of the present healthcare system, the emerging problems, and the methods for improving healthcare with an objective of providing affordable, accessible, and quality healthcare to the entire cross-section of our society.

The team has identified the imperatives for eradication of three major diseases—tuberculosis, HIV/AIDS, and water-borne diseases by the next decade. There are several others like cardiovascular diseases, neuro-psychiatric disorders, renal diseases and hypertension, gastro-intestinal disorders, eye disorders, genetic diseases, and accidents and trauma, which would require our attention. It is also realised that prosthodontic dental healthcare needs to be included in the Health Vision, as well.

We should explore the advancements in technology for improving the healthcare system in the country, in order to cope with such problems. Such an effort would make cost-effective medical technology and devices available and accessible to all. Figure 5.2 gives the core technologies required to be persued to provide health for all.

There is an urgent need for a unified approach to the planning of healthcare delivery in our country. Besides traditional medical education and research programmes, emphasis must be laid on polyclinic-level training programmes in clinical technologies. Indigenisation of expensive diagnostic and curative equipment, to make them cost-effective, and the establishment of a nationwide

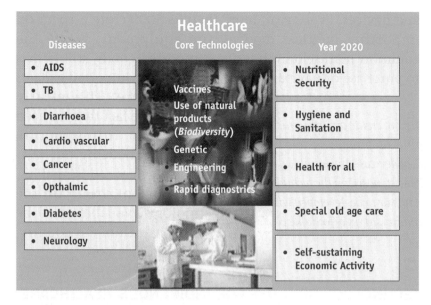

▲ **Fig. 5.2** *Healthcare*

maintenance mechanism of medical equipment using indigenous skills and spares is equally important. The cost of drugs needs to be brought down by scientifically developing herbal formulations and validating their effectiveness through clinical database, in addition to the allopathic route. Efforts made to integrate technology with healthcare can deliver the sought results to every corner of India.

NEED FOR INDIGENOUS MEDICAL TECHNOLOGY, DEVICES AND SYSTEMS

Not only for the 26% of the Indian population below the poverty line, even for the middle income group, medical care has not become affordable. A major problem in the Indian healthcare delivery system is the near total dependency on medical imports of diagnostic and therapeutic equipment and devices. Every year, more than Rs 5000 crore is spent on importing medical devices and equipment. While the common man seldom buys any imported goods, still he has to purchase or pay partly for the cost of the imported gadgets for healthcare. This clearly highlights the fact that we need to create an infrastructure capable of producing our own medical devices, consumables, and equipment, based on the technology available or to be developed within the country, at an affordable cost.

> *We need to create an infrastructure capable of producing our own medical devices, consumables, and equipment, based on the technology available or to be developed within the country, at an affordable cost.*

TECHNOLOGY SPIN-OFF FOR INDIGENOUS HEALTHCARE

The Society for Biomedical Technology (SBMT), an inter-ministerial initiative, was born to utilise research and technology spin-offs from research laboratories to bring healthcare within the reach of the common man. Some of the spin-offs from defence technologies are FRO, Cardiac stent, *Anamica*, Aspheric lens, *Drishti*, Typhoid Test Kit, Cytoscan, Dental implants, Hip joint, *Sanjeevani*, etc. (Fig. 5.3).

Standard Modular *Floor Reaction Orthosis* (FRO), a walking aid for polio-affected children was developed in a modular form in various standard sizes. The use of state-of-the-art composite materials and processes made FRO durable, strong, light weight (300 g) and less expensive (Rs. 300/-) as compared to the conventional caliper (weight ~3000 g and cost ~Rs. 1000/-). FRO is currently being produced by the Ministry of Social Justice and Empowerment in standard sizes and is used by many polio-affected children.

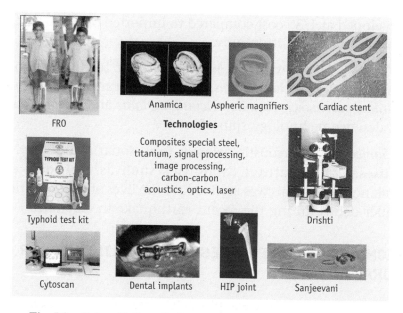

FRO

Anamica   Aspheric magnifiers   Cardiac stent

Technologies

Composites special steel,
titanium, signal processing,
image processing,
carbon-carbon
acoustics, optics, laser

Typhoid test kit

Drishti

Cytoscan   Dental implants   HIP joint   Sanjeevani

▲ **Fig. 5.3** *Spin-offs from Defence Technologies*

Coronary artery stents were hitherto imported at high cost. Introduction of indigenous stents made from the material used in defence projects, helped to bring down the cost. After clinical trials, the technology was transferred to a private entrepreneur for mass production and is being produced at one third of the cost of the imported stent. Many cardiac patients have been fitted with the indigenous stent.

Anamica is a spin-off product of the image processing technology. This is a medical visualisation software used to convert the 2D MRI/CT Scan pictures into 3D form, enabling the doctors to simulate the surgery on their computers. This software gives a better understanding of the tumour before the actual surgery is carried out, thus reducing the mortality rate.

Aspheric magnifier, a spin-off of optics is useful for improving the vision of the visually impaired. *Drishti*—an ophthalmic laser (Nd-Yag) photo disruptor known as Drishti-1064, developed at 1/3rd cost compared to imported one, is used for capsulotomy and iridotomy.

The *Typhoid Test Kit* is being used for testing typhoid infection at any place. *Cytoscan* (for early cancer detection), *Cardiac pacemaker, Titanium Dental implants* and *hip joints* are all defence technology spin-offs.

Sanjeevani, an acoustic detector from sonar technology, is a lifesaver in natural calamities such as earthquakes, avalanches, etc. This was used to save the lives of people buried under debris during the recent earthquake in Gujarat.

TECHNOLOGY-DRIVEN INTEGRATED HEALTHCARE FOR RURAL INDIA

Prof. M R Raju, a nuclear physicist, specialised in radiation oncology from Los Almos Laboratory in USA. After living for 35 years in the US, he returned to his native village, Peddamiram, near Bhimavaram in West Godavari district of Andhra Pradesh. Driven by a societal mission of self-sustaining villages, he created a computerised data bank of all individuals living within five kilometres of his village. The data, primarily on health parameters, provides other social, economic, and administrative details, which are imperative to the delivery of healthcare. Besides creating the data bank, Prof. Raju is providing integrated healthcare to the needy villagers.

We feel that the results of Prof. Raju's experiment in a rural area should spread. Multiple organisations must become active collaborators in this mission.

The major task of life science laboratories is to evolve and ensure optimal health, combat capability and operational efficiency irrespective of environmental conditions, be it high altitude, desert, underwater, or aerospace environment. The time is just ripe to integrate, through IT, the various aspects of the Indian healthcare system—diagnostics, curative procedures, drug therapy, preventive medicine, public health delivery, indigenous medicine, and clinical research.

> *The time is just ripe to integrate the various aspects of the Indian healthcare system through IT.*

An integrated medical informatics system has recently been developed and installed in some Indian hospitals. Work has commenced on the digitisation of medical images and their transmission over distances through existing communication infrastructure for real-time diagnosis by medical experts. Upgraded versions of these experiments, by developing our own medical technology on a national scale, will provide a solid platform for treating our millions.

Mobile Clinics in Rural Areas

TIFAC, along with the Government of Uttaranchal and Birla Institute of Scientific Research, has installed a mobile clinic at Almora, to provide medical assistance to the people in remote corners of the hilly regions. The mobile clinic is equipped with modern medical facilities, including X-ray, ECG, ultrasound, blood testing and other diagnostic equipment with a team of doctors, radiologists and paramedics. Also, the mobile van is fitted with audio-visual healthcare facilities for educating the rural people. Such mobile clinics must get networked with urban hospitals, providing electronic connectivity through satellite terminals. This will become a boon to the rural populace who are unreachable and cannot afford even the basic medical facilities.

Pharmaceutical Trends

The Indian Pharma Sector commenced operations with repacking and preparation of formulations from imported bulk drugs, but it has now moved on to become a net foreign exchange earner with the capability of producing more than 400 bulk drugs within the country. From a mere processing industry, it has grown into an advanced sector with advanced manufacturing technologies, modern equipment, stringent quality control developing products and at an affordable price. It is the time the pharma industry to envisage a vision for making India number one in the production of drugs from the present position of fourth in terms of volume and thirteenth in terms of value in the next two decades.

TECHNOLOGY AND TRADITIONAL HERBS

The world over traditional medicine has been practised for several centuries by different sects of people. The traditional systems of medicine like *Ayurveda*, *Sidha*, etc. have advocated and practised preventive and curative medicinal recipies. The body, mind, food and environment were looked at holistically to suggest a preventive or curative approach to health. The sciences of traditional medicine are different from those practised in modern allopathy. However, if we can interplay both sciences, it would have an impact on all societies.

New technologies, as evidenced by human genome sequencing, protemics, chemogenomics, ultra-high throughput screening, are revolutionising drug discovery. Medicinal plants too offer enormous scope for development of drugs. Seven important medicinal plants short-listed by the Scientific Advisory Committee of the cabinet are given in Fig. 5.4. These medicinal plants are important, in view of their application as drugs and economic value. Such medicinal plants can be systematically grown in Herbal gardens, and a species-wise layout of a typical herbal garden is given in Fig. 5.5. The modern tools in biotechnology can be used to prove the specific bioactivity of a medicinal plant, before it is used as a pharmaceutical product (Fig. 5.6). Centre for Biotechnology, Anna University proposes to create a database of traditional medicinal plants for specific bioactivity. 100 medicinal plants are being screened and leads for the development of new drugs have been obtained.

It is time traditional healers should think of using modern approaches to validate their products which will prove beneficial in approaching the groups of people who think adversely of traditional healers. Also this validation of biological action will prove immensely useful in marketing their products to a wider population.

Aloe vera
(*Ghrita kumari*)
Frostbites, burns, wounds

Rauwolfia serpentina
(*sarpagandha*)
Tranquilizing and
Anti-hypertensive effects

Centella asiatica
(*Mandookparni*)
Pain relief, Epilepsy
Schizophrenia

Bacopa monnieri
(*Brahmi*)
Retention,
Calming effect

Taxus baccata
(*Himalayan yew*)
Anti-cancer

Artemisia annua
Anti-drug resistant Malaria

Catharanthus roseus
(*Periwinkle*)
Treatment of
Leukemia

▲ **Fig. 5.4 *Important Medicinal Plants***

In addition, such tools can be exploited by traditional healers to control the quality of their preparations even

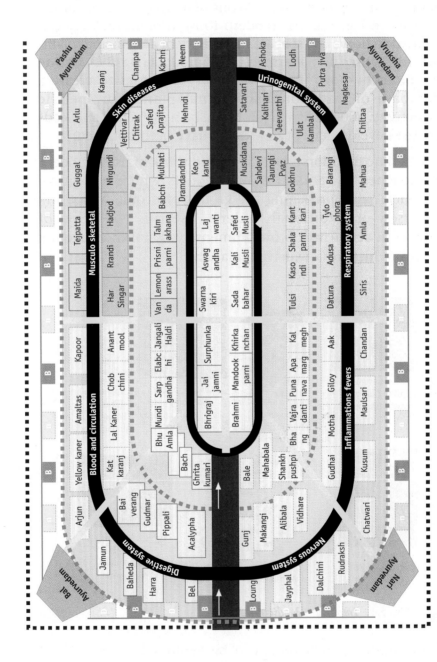

Fig. 5.5 *A Typical Herbal Garden Layout*

before the formulation of the product. As it is well-known, the bioactivity in medicinal plants varies according to seasonal patterns, soil conditions, etc. and therefore it is essential to employ quality checks on the products as soon as they are prepared.

The availability of these bioactivity-based screens in biotechnology can thus prove invaluable to traditional healers.

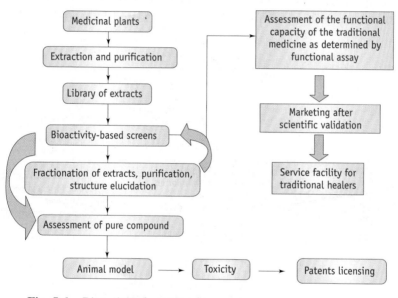

▲ **Fig. 5.6** *Bioactivity-based Screen*

CHALLENGES IN THE AREA OF HERBS

Our approach should be to exploit the knowledge, based on several molecules which play a significant role in normal cellular functions.

Most of these molecules including several signal switches, transporters on cell surfaces, adhesion molecules and other functional surface molecules, specific enzymes, etc. have been studied by the molecular and cell biological techniques. These could be used as targets and also as screening tools for bioactivity (Fig. 5.7). This approach of using functional bio-assays as screening templates may be the best way to determine specific biological activity. Further this could enable the rapid isolation of the active molecules, leading to structural elucidation. For this approach to succeed, an interface between cell biology, *in vitro* assays, and structural chemistry will be required to obtain valuable leads.

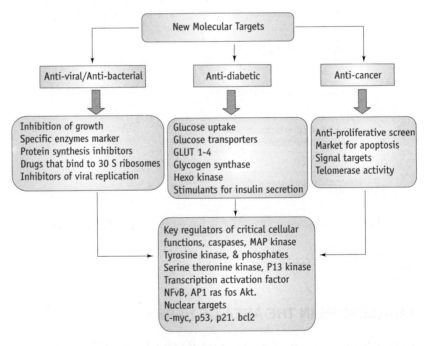

▲ **Fig. 5.7   *New Molecular Targets***

The approach to convert a molecule to drug has been shown in Fig. 5.8. The database on bioinformatics is generated through the studies on mammalian cell culture *in vitro*, molecular and cell biology, and botanical leads. The information from this database is extracted to fix and solve a specific problem related to healthcare. The problem is examined and screened thoroughly using biotechnological screening tool and is fixed at the molecular level. After the identification and fixing of the problem, a suitable drug is designed to solve it. Again research and development is carried out for the design of the drug at the molecular level. This involves convergence of expertise in pharmaceutical sciences, pharmacology characterisation facility, *in vitro* test facility, clinical facility and a sponsor for financing the developmental work.

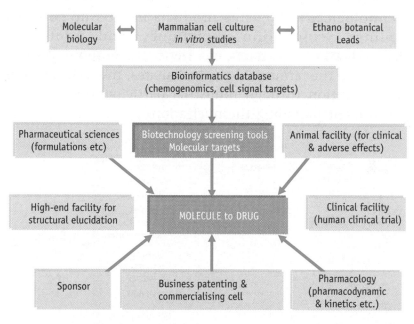

▲ **Fig. 5.8** *Molecule to Drug*

Using this approach, Anna University has identified three new anti-cancer molecules and two anti-diabetic molecules, which are at different levels of analyses and may yield valuable drugs.

A model of Incubation Centres (IC) for herbal products have been evolved (Fig. 5.9) as an example of garnering natural resources and native knowledge towards creating wealth. It evolved as a result of the follow-up action on the SAC-C (Scientific Advisory Committee to the Cabinet) recommendations. The ICs would synergise the efforts of the Indian herbal industries to make a place for themselves in the global market. These ICs are being created with the aim of providing business resources and professional services towards rendering technology support to Indian herbal industries that are predominantly in the small-scale sector. The product line from these ICs would therefore be semi-finished in nature and would be more in the forum of technologically-intensive products like tissue cultured saplings, cultivation techniques and protocols, standardisation of extracts, etc. Hence the purpose of ICs is to bring to the farmers, in the herbal area, the techniques of value addition through industrial participation, with the government providing the nucleation.

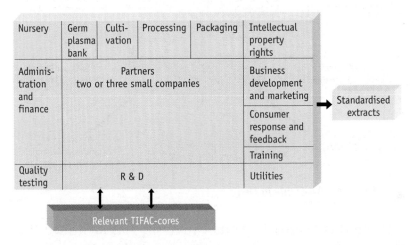

Fig. 5.9   *Incubation Centre for Herbal Products: A Model*

AN EXPERIENCE TO REMEMBER: HERBAL MEDICINE

We would like to narrate an incident here about how devoted healthcare and native herbal system resulted in curing frostbite completely. DRDO has a laboratory in the upper hills of Himachal Pradesh called the Snow and Avalanche Study Establishment (SASE). This establishment has outstation observatories at altitudes of 15,000 and 19,000 ft. Recently, a team of scientists was moving from one station to another when they encountered a snow blizzard. Though most of the team members escaped unharmed, one of them got trapped in the snow. When he was rescued after two days, he had developed severe Grade IV frostbite in the feet and arms.

The doctors at local hospital suggested to amputate the affected parts. Subsequently, the Delhi-based DRDO laboratory, Defence Institute of Physiology and Allied Sciences (DIPAS) was entrusted with the responsibility of providing healthcare through the use of an Indian herbal extract *Aloe Vera* along with allopathic treatment. DIPAS took it as a challenge and worked with the patient. The effort bore fruit and resulted in the complete recovery of the patient within 45 days of treatment, without any amputation. Faith in the Indian herbal system was restored!

The experience brings out the tremendous potential of the Indian herbal system in combating various ailments, and also the patient–doctor relationship. We would like to suggest that doctors and medical specialists look at patients as integrated human beings or psycho-physiological entities, and for whom the treatment has to be multifaceted. Certain diseases can be cured through the Indian system alone while others may require a combination of Indian and allopathic systems, with reference to the condition of the patient.

BIOTECHNOLOGY

Biotechnology has made tremendous growth, particularly in the fields of DNA techniques, cell and tissue culture, immunology, enzymology, bioprocess engineering, and vaccinology. The discovery of DNA and its use in cloning adult mammals has opened-up new vistas earlier unheard of. The availability of new biotechnological tools and the production of microbes, plants, and animals with improved traits have opened-up opportunities for better products and processes. Notable developments in this field include, immuno diagnostics—development of diagnostic kits for the early detection of a variety of communicable and non-communicable diseases:

- Crop biotechnology—genetic engineering for gene isolation, transformation, etc. to facilitate agricultural productivity

- Animal biotechnology—the main areas of research are embryo transfer technology, healthcare and diagnostics, nutrition, genetic resource conservation, leather biotechnology, and development of bioproducts

- Aquaculture—feed development, production of transgenic fish, extraction of bio-active compounds, cryo preservation of embryos, and development of disease diagnostics

- Biofertilisers—biological control of plant pests, diseases and weeds

- Industrial biotechnology—gene cloning, biotech-nological methods for the enrichment of ores, and pro-duction processes for edible mushrooms.

In India, development of biotechnology has been spearheaded by the Department of Biotechnology, and certain states have taken the initiative for creating a 'Vision Group for Biotechnology' and are ensuring a single window clearance for biotechnology projects. The strengths and opportunities in the field of biotechnology in India are mentioned in Fig. 5.10.

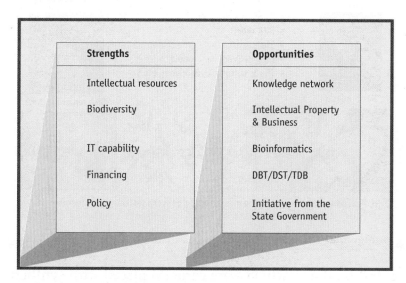

Strengths	Opportunities
Intellectual resources	Knowledge network
Biodiversity	Intellectual Property & Business
IT capability	Bioinformatics
Financing	DBT/DST/TDB
Policy	Initiative from the State Government

▲ **Fig. 5.10 *Biotechnology in India***

Another area, which has emerged is bioinformatics or the application of IT for the collation, organisation, and analyses of large amounts of biological data arising from the human genome project, genomics, and drug chemistry. Recent initiatives in this area include the setting-up of 52 bioinformation centres across the country by the Department of Biotechnology and the setting-up of Bioinformatic Centre near Bangalore by TIFR.

In the future, biologically catalysed processes for production of fine organic chemicals and pharmaceuticals will be a force to reckon with. Bio-engineering systems will be used to dispose hazardous waste and also generate valuable by-products. Further, as a result of genetic engineering, many

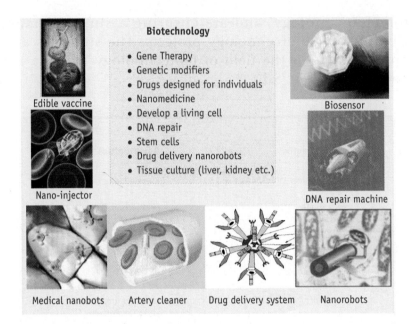

▲ **Fig. 5.11** *Biotechnology*

natural products, which were earlier replaced with synthetic substitutes would reappear. Biosensors are also likely to be used extensively to monitor environmental pollution or blood analysis or identify a fruit's ripeness. Nanomedicine genetic modifiers, advanced drug delivery systems, tissue culture, DNA repair, etc. are the future challenges (Fig. 5.11). The technologies for bringing these to fruitation include bio-catalysis, bioengineering systems, biomolecular materials, and bio-materials.

Biosensor

At Anna University, a doctoral research project is currently under way to find a software/hardware integrated solution to achieve a near normal functioning of the brain of the mentally challenged children. Convergence of information and communication technology, medical electronics, biotechnology and mathematical simulation can find a solution to this problem. By transforming the functions of the damaged portion of the brain to the normal portion of the brain and implanting a bio-chip can solve this problem. The research still continues!

Stem Cell Research

The recent identification and characterisation of progenitors with stem cell properties have opened new avenues that may be useful for treating functional impairments caused by the death of specific cell population. Stem cells may help restore the functioning of certain defective organs, by repopulating or rescuing the damaged cells from further degeneration. This would lead to a revolution in the medical treatment for heart diseases, cancer, blindness and the mentally challenged. It is essential to launch an integrated national stem cell research programme.

Biotechnology will also be the predominant technology in the agricultural field in the years to come. One of the important technologies to look out for is the development of transgenic plants, i.e., plants tailored to meet the desired objective by the transfer and expression of the desired type of gene(s).

In India, biotechnology and bioinformatics have a good scope including high throughput screening for new chemical entities, genomics and pharmaco-genomics, gene therapy, diagnostic kits, bio-pesticides and bio-fertilisers, industrial enzymes, and environmental biotech products.

Vaccines Development

An area which can lead to heightened healthcare is research into the development of vaccines for dreaded diseases like AIDS and Malaria. HIV virus, the cause of AIDS, has reached alarming proportions and at present in India there are around 4 million people estimated to be affected by this virus. In India, a prototype of the candidate virus is under development and is ready for pre-clinical toxicological studies.

Another area which needs attention is malaria which kills more than 1 million people each year in the world. Research is on for developing a vaccine by following a method of double dosage—with initial vaccination from the malarial parasite followed by a dose of harmless virus containing different malarial DNA. This has been found to produce 5 to 10 times anti-malaria T Cells responsible for killing the virus.

REDESIGNING AND TRANSFORMING HEALTHCARE

Rapid developments are taking place almost on a daily basis in the healthcare delivery worldwide. The combined impact of new revolutionary technologies, advanced management practices, and the evolving political and social climate of medicine have created a host of transformations influencing the mode and means of healthcare delivery. The redesigning of healthcare institutions is also leading to reshaping of the hospital as the main mode of healthcare delivery. Other institutions in the healthcare environment are also undergoing radical modifications. All these are creating challenges and opportunities for researchers and practitioners in 'bringing technology, healthcare, and management together (Fig. 5.11).' We will have to gather researchers who are exploring bridging the three components (Disease prevention, diagnosis and treatment) of healthcare delivery—with an eye towards the future—and practitioners who are interested in these topics.

Disease prevention	Technology for diagnosis	Technology for treatment
• Sanitation • Drinking water • Education • Vaccination	• **Instrument for Blood picture and Blood pressure** • **Imaging of body:** X-ray, ultrasound & colour doppler, CT scan, NMRI, functional NMRI, PET (Positron Emission Tomography) Nuclear imaging + video imaging, angiographies	❏ **Intervention Technologies** Enter inside the body: angioplastry and cardiac stent
		❏ **Brachytherapy** ▪ Targeting the organs using radiation ▪ Laproscopic operation without cutting ▪ Robotics surgery: remote control of operation
• Population screening for infectious disease		❏ **Prosthetic** Replacement of parts like heart valves/dental implants (orthodontics) ❏ **Immune systems** in which research is under progress

▲ **Fig. 5.11** *Technological Needs for Healthcare* ▪▪

In the future the following areas will gain significance in the healthcare sector:

1. *Management of technology in healthcare organisations:* nature of work and skills in healthcare delivery; processes and performance; knowledge management in healthcare; strategies for technological positioning in hospitals; managed care and cost controls; uses of technology in primary care; logistics, infrastructure, and architecture of the hospital of the future.

2. *Management and organisation of information technology in healthcare organisations:* applications and processes in the implementation and diffusion of IT in healthcare; role of standards in communication and organisation; networking through IT; computerised medical records.

3. *Organisation, management, and applications of emerging medical technologies, e-health, telehealth,*

and telemedicine: role of these emerging technologies; processes, barriers, and organisational issues in the implementation and adoption of these technologies.

The advent of communication technology has made telemedicine a popular means of treatment. By using telemedicine it is possible to connect remote villages to major hospitals wherein a patient's condition is diagnosed by a doctor in the hospital and his views communicated through the communication link. One such system has been installed at Care Hospital in Hyderabad which has been linked to a village in Mahboobnagar District (Fig. 5.12).

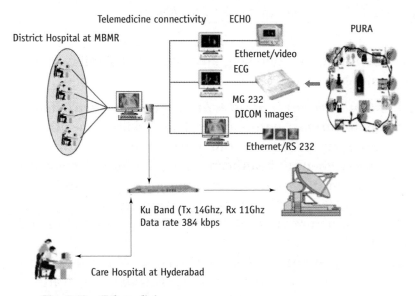

Fig. 5.12   *Telemedicine*

4. *Medical technologies and patient value*: value contribution of medical technologies to patients; the role of patient confidentiality in view of technological developments; ethical issues; healthcare technologies and medical outcomes; the role of standards, regulations, government, and their impacts on medical technologies and the value to patients.

5. *Medical technologies and emergency medicine*: how healthcare and medical technologies contribute and will continue to contribute to emergency medicine; crisis healthcare delivery; and healthcare in catastrophic situations.

Innovations introduced in the 1990s have created accumulated effects that will be compounded with the continuing technological progress in medicine. Areas such as telemedicine, telehealth, computerised medical records, e-health, and use of the Internet in B2B and B2C applications in healthcare are some of the milestones which are revamping the healthcare landscape. Thus, a key ingredient in this age of challenge and transformation is the redesign of the hospital as the ideal provider of care. Already the innovations in the medical and healthcare technologies are transforming the operation, design, and mission of hospitals.

HEALTHCARE INDUSTRY

The healthcare industry is on the threshold of a major growth spiral, which shall assimilate all new technologies to provide cost-effective healthcare. It is poised to

> *The healthcare industry is poised to become the biggest employer in all countries.*

become the biggest employer in all countries and shall not only employ the largest chunk of all available capital but also a large proportion of the skilled workforce. It shall also become the biggest consumer of all new technologies.

The healthcare industry must adapt itself to absorb new technologies to meet the challenges in the times ahead. It must address the following in a planned manner:

1. Deployment of microprocessor technology to develop implantable devices, which can be monitored with remote sensors. These devices shall be used by healthcare providers for overcoming various physiological defects in patients.

2. A greater degree of deployment of CPU-driven technology, supported with artificial intelligence, for treating or managing various physiological defects.

3. Deployment of robotics technology in operating rooms to provide precise and less traumatic, as well as, less destructive surgery (robotic micro-surgery).

4. A greater degree of the use of robotics technology in laboratories, along with traditional technologies to provide automated and precise diagnostic studies.

5. A greater degree of the use of laser technology, inside and outside the operating rooms, to provide precise and less traumatic, as well as, less destructive surgery.

6. Development and deployment of instrumentation in medical and surgical practices, based on capturing real-time data and providing necessary electro-physiological interventions or biochemical intervention. This shall affect both normal and pathological physiology.

7. Development and deployment of cultured tissues for control of vital biological processes.

8. Using IT tools for networking examination rooms, treatment rooms, operating rooms, and diagnostic reporting room.

9. Using IT tools, along with microprocessor technologies and modules of Artificial Intelligence, for maintenance of equipment and other instruments remotely thereby enabling development of remote controlled instrumentation for the control of physiological and pathological processes.

10. Deployment of IT tools for the generation of specific disease related databases, classified by a number of variables.

NETWORKING THE INSTITUTIONS

It is essential for the technologists to work for an 'Integrated Health For All' in a mission mode, which can be suitably evolved for implementation. The mission may include the following:

- Networking of medical universities, institutions, R&D laboratories, industries and social organisations in key areas like assistance to the handicapped and the disabled.

- Launching awareness-cum-preventive programmes to check the growing incidence of TB and cancer.

- Creation of a nation wide cold storage chain for polio and other temperature-sensitive vaccines.

- Conducting hospital-linked diploma courses on medical technology maintenance at the state technical educational institutions.

- Establishment of an industry-supported system for maintenance and upgradation of medical equipment.

- Productionisation of selective assistive devices, like hearing aids, and medical consumables like electrodes, catherters and leads.

CONCLUDING REMARKS

Healthcare is an important sector in the vision of developed India, providing tremendous opportunities for using bio-diversity, intellectual resources, IT and knowledge network, bioinformatics, and spin-offs from space, defence and nuclear technologies for societal missions.

Healthcare technology has evolved in the past few decades to provide unprecedented assistance in diagnosis and treatment. It is essential for the government and non-governmental agencies to evolve a well-established process for knowledge acquisition, dissemination and knowledge absorption by people. The knowledge society is unfolding, spreading light over the darkest corners of human ignorance and misdemeanour. In the knowledge-driven economy and society, with education, healthcare and proper occupation, responsible citizenship is born. That will pave the way for a prosperous nation with a stabilised population. An integrated mission of rural development evolved by multiple departments with industrial partners and social institutions is also needed.

India ranks among the top few nations having rich bio-diversity. In the herbal area there are potential applications for developing multiple products for nutrition, prevention and cure of diseases. Of the global herbal product market of US$ 61 billion, China has a share of around US $ 6 billion, whereas India's share is not even US $ 1 billion. There are tremendous opportunity for growth in this area. India has similar potential for promoting floriculture and aquaculture in a big way. Knowledge-based value addition for these natural resources would mean exporting value-added products rather than merely the raw materials. The use of IT for commercialisation and marketing can increase our reach and speed enormously.

Indian biotechnologists with business houses will have opportunity of analysing the available genomic data, leading to production of drugs for healthcare and treatment. Bioresearch transforming into technology will lead to higher production of agricultural products. Biotechnology has got tremendous potential in providing pest free agriculture production with genetically modified seeds to increase productivity.

The growth of the healthcare industry should be supported by political will and social understanding, at all levels of any society. It must, therefore, meet emerging challenges by providing 'cost-effective' healthcare in a manner that improves the quality of human life. The aim is to achieve health for all by 2020. NGOs can assist and enrich our land by introducing mobile clinics for different village clusters. Like healthcare sector, revolution in strategic technologies have made many significant impact in the human life and security of the Nations.

6

Advances in the Strategic Sector

INTRODUCTION

Technology plays an important role in the development of critical systems. This chapter examines the present technology level in the strategic sector comprising of aeronautics, space, defence and nuclear energy, the strides made till now, and the systems likely to dominate in the future. It also discusses the various state-of-the-art technologies developed by India in the course of various aerospace programmes. The future aerospace profile for 2020 like passenger aircraft, advanced GSLVs and PSLVs, hypersonic reusable vehicles, mission to planets, etc. have also been highlighted.

Supersonic Cruise Missile BRAHMOS takes off from a Naval warship

" The nation's ability to provide its own security and to conduct an independent foreign policy is dependent on the degree to which the nation is able to underpin self-reliance in defence and defence systems "

WAR THROUGH THE AGES

The Indian civilisation has undergone centuries of intercenine warfare and external invasions. Some of the invaders took away our wealth, others took away our culture, and still others implanted new cultures. It is an astonishing fact that the Indian civilisation has been dynamically regenerating itself through all these wars. It is indeed the greatness of the Indian society that India was able to amalgamate multiple ways of life and thinking. There have not many Indian emperors in our history of 3000 years, who had invaded other nations and ruled them. India has not subjugated any nation.

There are two schools of thought, as to why this did not happen. One group says that Indians are tolerant and absorbed others cultures. Another group feels that it was due to deficiencies in our thought-process, coupled with inadequacy of the state-of-the-art weaponry.

Currently subjugation of India continues in many forms by other countries—through commercially motivated information medium. We need to consider whether we should inculcate a different way of thinking. Winning a war and defending the nation are directly proportional to strategic thinking and weaponry (Fig. 6.1).

In this situation, a nation like India is facing globalisation of the market place and patent regimes armed with technology controls. This is a new type of invasion from the developed world. The only answer is technological strength focused through vision and a consortium of like-minded countries.

Factors	Human warfare	Weapon warfare	Economic warfare 
Motivator	Religion/ territory	Ideology/ domination	Technological superiority
Theatre of war	Land, sea	Air space, under water	Global markets cyberspace 
Means of domination	Human and animal strength	Weapon strength and numerical superiority	Technological monopoly
			Globalisation of markets
			Economic enslavement of weaker nations

▲   **Fig. 6.1**   *War Through the Ages*

EVOLUTION OF WAR WEAPONRY

The evolution of rocket in modern warfare is said to have started from India. Prof. R Narasimha brought out a small and authentic book on this subject. His research on the Srirangapatna battle of 1792, shows that war rockets were deployed to defeat the British cavalry (Fig. 6.2). Now, Indian rocketry has taken tremendous strides through ISRO and DRDO.

In the years 1920–90, remarkable progress has been made in war weaponry with new platforms and high technology intelligent and autonomous systems. This was not because

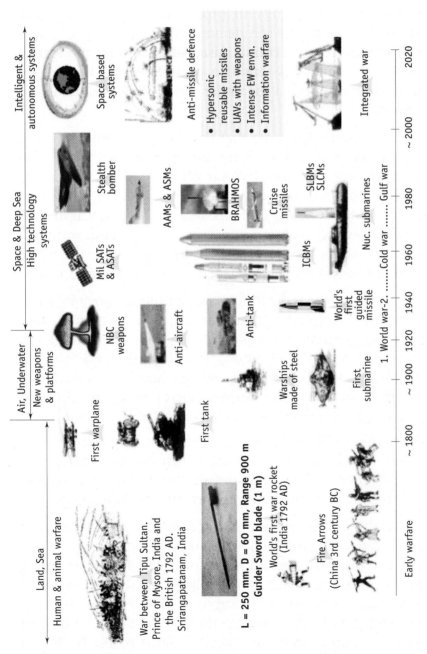

Fig. 6.2 *Evolution of War Weaponry*

of love for technology or progress, but because of the ideological clash between democracy professed by USA and allied countries and communism advocated by the former Soviet Union. This was the period when the best of technologies emerged for under water, air, space, and land combat.

It is important to note that the European nations fought for 100 years with each other and precipitated two World Wars. During the Second World War, nuclear weapons were deployed on two cities of Japan, killing lakhs of people and permanently disabling millions. During the cold war nuclear submarines and precision missiles carrying nuclear warheads in large numbers were produced. Unfortunately, the world does not know how to eliminate the nuclear warheads totally.

A strong desire to have supremacy in technology by some countries, coupled with economic development led to technology denials and control regimes, separating the Nations into 'Developed', 'Developing' and 'Under-developed'. Now, the world is facing a new kind of warfare—an integrated situation arising out of religious conflicts, ideological differences and economic-market warfare.

During 1990–2000, a transformation took place with technology emerging as a tool, which can be used for the development of the nation and also for defence. It is evident that technology has found its way into multiple fields.

On the economic front, technology will transform healthcare, food production, IT and manufacturing. World will also witness international planetary flights for exploring new habitats in space. Anti-ballistic missile systems and space-based systems are going to dominate future warfare. The collapse of the former Soviet Union and the South-East Asian economic crash are directly related to the birth of a single superpower and the dollar governance of the global market. Globally, only two giants are emerging: the industrially strong Japan with its technological foundation and the integrated European Union through its Euro currency and its focus on injecting the concept of consortium of industries with technology focus.

NUCLEAR PROGRAMME OF INDIA

India's nuclear energy programme has two components. One is to enable capability for making the nation strong, in view of the security threats. The second is to develop and utilise nuclear energy for applications such as power generation, and in agriculture, medicine, industry and other areas.

India's nuclear programme was spearhead by Dr. H J Bhabha. He assembled around him a gifted team of young scientists and engineers from many fields. When *Apsara*, India's first nuclear research reactor was made critical five decades ago, India entered the nuclear age. The three stage programme, charted by Dr. H J Bhabha for the power sector aimed at establishing nuclear power with resources comprising of the following guidelines:

(a) First stage—use of natural uranium in pressurised heavy water reactors and the production of power and plutonium

(b) Second stage—use of recycled fuel from the first stage combined with plutonium produced in fast breeder reactors, and

(c) Third stage—use of thorium-233 in an advanced fuel cycle.

The maximum potential from first stage is estimated to be 10,000 MWe and the second stage is estimated to be 3,50,000 MWe. The potential of the third stage is significantly higher and about six times that of the second stage.

First Stage Programme

At present the first stage programme is in progress and has reached a stage of maturity. The present nuclear power generation is about 3000 MW. There are fourteen reactors in operation that includes 2 Boiling Water Reactors (BWR) and 12 Pressurized Heavy Water Reactors (PWHR) as given in table below:

Location	Type/Capacity
Tarapur	BWR/2 × 160 MWe
Rajasthan	PHWR/1 × 100, 1 × 200 MWe and 2 × 220 MWe
Kalpakkam	PHWR/2 × 170 MWe
Narora	PHWR/2 × 220 MWe
Kakrapara	PHWR/2 × 220 MWe
Kaiga	2 PHWR units of 220 MWe

The nuclear programme has eight power reactors under construction at present with a total installed capacity of 3960 MWe. The table given below summarizes the Nuclear Power reactors under construction.

Location	Type/Capacity	Expected Criticality Date
Tarapur (3 & 4)	PHWR/2 × 540 MWe	• Unit 3 – July 2006 • Unit 4 – Oct 2005
Kaiga (3 & 4)	PHWR/2 × 220 MWe	• Unit 3 – Dec 2006 • Unit 4 – June 2007
Rajasthan (5 & 6)	PHWR/2 × 220 MWe	• Unit 5 – May 2007 • Unit 6 – Nov 2007
Kudankulam, Tamil Nadu	LWR/2 × 1000 MWe	• Unit 1 – 2007 • Unit 2 – 2008

Second and Third Stage Programmes

A beginning has been made on the second stage programme with the sanction of construction of 500 MWe PFBR (Prototype Fast Breeder Reactor) in the Tenth Plan. This is expected to be followed by a number of FBRs. When the capacity through FBRs builds up to reasonable level, the deployment of Thorium through third stage will begin and be realised in the long term. However, as a part of technology demonstration to utilise thorium for electricity generation, a 300 MWe Advanced Heavy Water Reactor (AHWR) is proposed to be taken up for construction in the Tenth Plan.

With this, the Department of Atomic Energy plans to put up a total installed nuclear power capacity of 20,000 MWe by the year 2020.

Research and Development

Dr. Homi Bhabha also established the Tata Institute of Fundamental Research (TIFR) and Atomic Research Centre at Trombay for advanced research in nuclear energy. Many leaders followed him and established a number of research centres and nuclear power stations. Bhabha Atomic Research Centre (BARC), the premier research centre of Department of Atomic Energy, (DAE) has been working closely with NPC in its rapid indigenisation tasks. BARC has developed comprehensive technology for industrial operation in fuel reprocessing and waste management. Another multidisciplinary R & D Centre, Indira Gandhi Centre for Atomic Research is dedicated to fast reactor technology and associated fuel cycle, material sciences, fuel reprocessing and sodium technology. One thing we would like to state is that India's nuclear programme is self-reliant in technologies.

Spin-Off Technologies

There have been many important spin-off technologies from the Indian nuclear programme such as super computing system ANUPAM, Robotic devices, radio isotope for treatment of cancer, radio pharmaceuticals, water treatment plants, irradiation for improved seeds and preservation of fruits and vegetables, detection of leaks in buried pipelines, a PC based scanjet digital scanner image capturing, processing and display system, etc. In addition, there have been considerably technology contributions in metallurgy, biotechnology and electronic areas.

SPACE MISSIONS OF INDIA

During the last 40 years, India has progressed tremendously in space, missiles, and multiple aircraft programmes. Visionary leaders like Dr. Vikram Sarabhai and Prof Satish Dhawan laid the strong foundation of space programme in India. Through the successful launching of SLV-3 in July 1980, India attained indigenous launch capability to inject low earth orbiting satellites and thereby became an exclusive member of the Space Club. Further the Augmented Satellite Launch Vehicle (ASLV) enhanced the capability to inject larger satellites for scientific experiments. Another major break-through in launch vehicle technology came with the launch of Polar Satellite Launch Vehicle (PSLV) capable of launching multiple satellites in a single mission for different countries.

The vision of Dr. Vikram Sarabhai —to use space technology for the development of the nation—has become a reality.

The recent launch of the Geosynchromons Satellite Launch Vehicle (GSLV), has established India's capability to orbit INSAT class of missions in geosynchronous orbit. The Indian Remote Sensing (IRS) satellite series provide high-resolution images, which are required for the management of natural resources. The application of remote sensing is many, as given in Fig. 6.3. The pictures from IRS provide details required for urban planning, agriculture, coastal land use, fishing zones, ground water resources, land conservation, mineral exploration, forest and environment protection and so on. The Indian National Satellite (INSAT) series also meet the communication, television, and meteorology demands of the country. With the PSLV operational and the GSLV shaping up, ISRO has established not only self-reliance in launch and satellite capability, but can also offer cost-effective launch

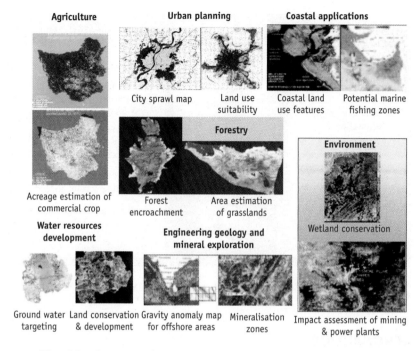

Agriculture

Urban planning

Coastal applications

City sprawl map   Land use suitability

Coastal land use features   Potential marine fishing zones

Forestry

Environment

Acreage estimation of commercial crop

Forest encroachment   Area estimation of grasslands

Wetland conservation

Water resources development

Engineering geology and mineral exploration

Ground water targeting   Land conservation & development   Gravity anomaly map for offshore areas   Mineralisation zones   Impact assessment of mining & power plants

▲   **Fig. 6.3**   *Space Applications*

services and build satellites for different countries. The vision of Dr. Sarabhai—to use space technology for the development of the nation—has become a reality. Space applications have a major role in the societal transformation. These include teleeducation, telemedicine and integrated healthcare, connectivity for community development. Solar power satellite for energy generation and desalination of water from ocean resources mining from other planets and space tourism. In the year 2020, space technology is expected to provide 100 million phone connections with 2 million V-SAT terminals, virtual organisations, real time universal language translation, etc. (Fig. 6.4).

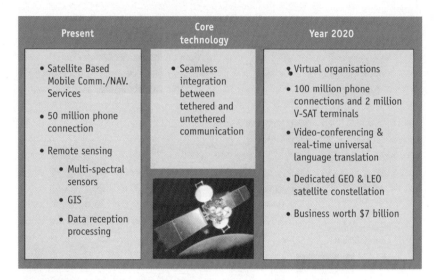

Present	Core technology	Year 2020

• Satellite Based Mobile Comm./NAV. Services
 	
• 50 million phone connection
 	
• Remote sensing
  • Multi-spectral sensors
  • GIS
  • Data reception processing
	• Seamless integration between tethered and untethered communication	• Virtual organisations
		
		• 100 million phone connections and 2 million V-SAT terminals
		
		• Video-conferencing & real-time universal language translation
		
		• Dedicated GEO & LEO satellite constellation
		
		• Business worth $7 billion

▲ **Fig. 6.4** *Space Communication and Remote Sensing*

AERONAUTICS

NAL flight-tested a small aircraft *Hansa*, and HAL flight-tested the Advanced Light Helicopter (ALH). The ALH is a unique, multi-role, state-of-the-art, cost-effective helicopter and will be a workhorse of Indian aviation in the coming years. It has composite structure with hingeless composite main rotor with elastomeric bearings, a bearing-less composite tail rotor, and crashworthy composite airframe that ensures longer life and low life-cycle cost.

DRDO's *Lakshya* and *Nishant* are unmanned aerial vehicles used as target and for reconnaissance respectively. The available MiG series of aircraft has been upgraded with avionics systems and new weapons, extending its life by 10 years in a cost-effective manner. For the aeronautical community, the real milestone was the successful demonstration flight of the prototypes of Light Combat Aircraft (LCA). The recent success of IJT by HAL is a notable achievement. The country today has design and development capability for civil, trainer and military aircraft. On the whole, the aerospace systems programme of India has achieved significant progress, as displayed in Fig. 6.5.

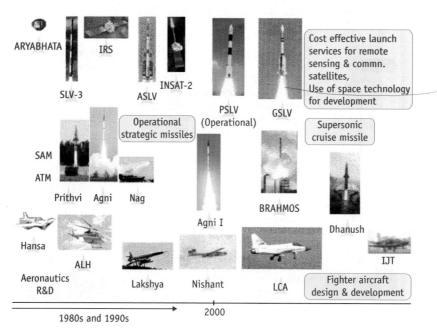

Fig. 6.5 *Aeronautics and Space Missions*

GUIDED MISSILE PROGRAMME OF INDIA

In the missile programme, India has made *Prithvi* and *Agni* operational as strategic missile systems. Prithvi is a short range surface-to-surface missile launched from a mobile launcher and uses liquid propellant rocket engine, light weight airframe, high accuracy strapdown inertial guidance system and electrohydraulic control system. *Prithvi* system has been inducted in the Indian Army. Soon *Prithvi* will get inducted in Air Force. *Dhanush*, the naval version of *Prithvi*, was successfully lauched from onboard a ship. *Agni* is an Intermediate Range Ballistic Missile has two versions. Specially developed carbon composite re-entry vehicle structure and re-entry guidance and control, solid propellant rocket motors, advanced guidance algorithms are the features of the IRBM. *Agni* is in the induction stage.

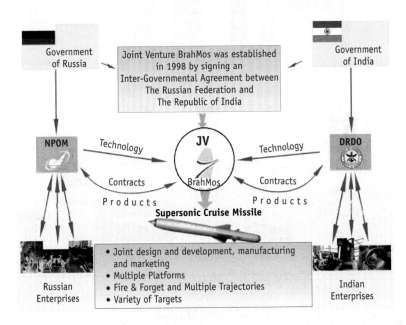

▲   **Fig. 6.6   *Joint Venture BrahMos***

We have recently seen a breakthrough in missile system, when BrahMos, an Indo-Russian joint venture supersonic cruise missile was launched successfully from an Indian warship in February 2003. This project harnesses the strengths of Indian missile technologies along with that of Russian institutes, proving to the world that a joint venture in advanced technology can lead to a high performance product with far-reaching capability in the shortest possible time. No other country (except India and Russia) has developed a **supersonic** cruise missile, of this class. Thus, India possesses a superior technology system, through this joint venture (Fig. 6.6).

AEROSPACE TECHNOLOGY STRENGTH

In the course of various aerospace programmes, India developed multiple state-of-the-art technologies (Fig. 6.7). Computational Fluid Dynamics (CFD) emerged as a core strength for India with advanced software codes and super-computing capability to optimize configurations for guided missiles, LCA, and launch vehicles. Expertise in CFD is available with Defence Research and Development Laboratory (DRDL), Vikram Sarabhai Space Centre (VSSC), National Aeronautical Laboratory (NAL), Aeronautical Development Agency (ADA), and IISc. CAD/CAM has become the order of the day for aerospace systems. ADA has established unique software capability for virtual reality, which reduces the design and product realisation time by 40%. Development of fibre optics and ring laser gyros with better accuracies, microprocessors, microwave components and devices, phase shifters, and onboard computers and the availability of silicon and gallium arsenide foundries for VLSI and MMIC components have helped India minimize its dependance on developed countries.

There are challenges in information technology, particularly related to software security. India seems to believe in proprietary solutions. The spread of IT and its influence in aerospace systems would have devastating effect due to any small shift in business practice involving these proprietary solutions, in a competitive environment. India should therefore introduce open source codes so that the aerospace community can build their own security algorithms.

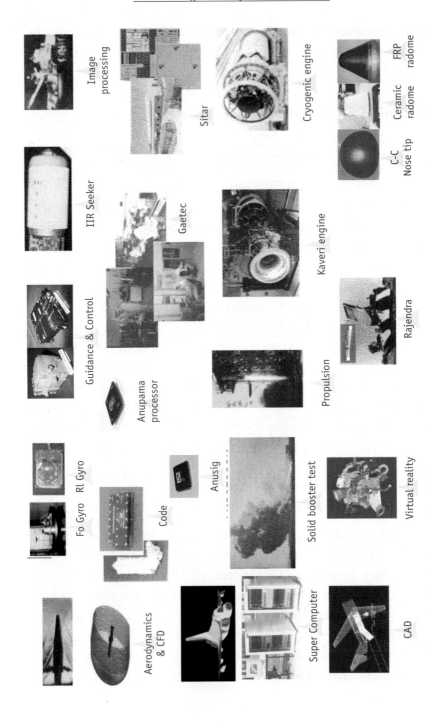

Fig. 6.7 Aerospace Technology Strength

In the area of propulsion, ISRO's large solid propellant rocket motor providing 500 tonnes of thrust, liquid propulsion in DRDL and Liquid Propulsions System Centre (LPSC), and the development effort of *Kaveri* and cryogenic engines established a sound base. In addition, the development of solid propellant Ramjet for *Akash* and the emergence of liquid Ramjet technology in BRAHMOS are of great importance in the development of highly efficient propulsion systems.

Kaveri is an 80 KN thrust class, twin-spool, low-bypass, augmented turbo fan engine. The engine incorporates the flat rating characteristics such that the usual thrust drop due to high ambient temperature/forward speed is compensated by suitable automatic control system features, which permit the raise of the turbine entry temperature as required. It also has a Full Authority Digital Engine Control System (FADECS) used for controlling dry engine operation, afterburner operation, and nozzle area operation. Success of Kaveri engine with advanced FADECS application in LCA for the air-force and navy, will lead to growth opportunity by exploring the use in passenger aircraft. A vectored nozzle can be added to meet the requirements of Medium Combat Aircraft and beyond.

The liquid propellant engine of *Prithvi* established high reliability in performance for different ranges with different payloads and is the main stay for *Prithvi* system. The energy level for each of the propulsion systems is measured in terms of Specific Impulse (Sec). Solid and liquid propellants provide 300 sec, cryogenics give 450 sec, solid Ramjet gives 600 sec, and the liquid Ramjet gives 1200 sec of specific impulse as shown in Fig. 6.8, along with the possible speed of the system in Mach number. Hence, the liquid Ramjet engine used in

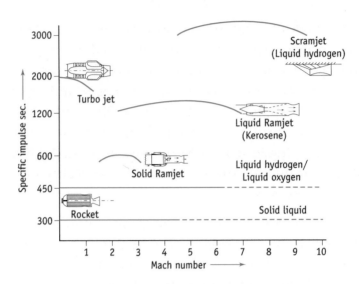

▲   **Fig. 6.8**   *Specific Impulse of Various Rocket Engines*

BRAHMOS has a definite advantage of four times of the energy level of solid propellants in addition to low weight, low volume, excellent fuel economy, and wide altitude of operation in supersonic cruise mode (Fig. 6.9). Further, BRAHMOS can be launched from multiple platforms including aircraft, ship, submarine, and from shore.

In composite technology, the carbon–carbon nose tip of *Agni* and high temperature radomes and large composite wing of LCA show the strength of the country. The digital fly-by-wire control system and the control laws developed for LCA rendered the aircraft state-of-the-art, in spite of sanctions by a developed country on the collaboration. This technology strength clearly shows that India could achieve multiple technologies using networking of academic institutions, R&D organisations, and industry driven by programmes. There could be some delays in realising some of the technologies but the Indian scientists who have chosen to live in India have demonstrated that they can develop critical technologies through indigenous effort and prove to those

Range – 290 km   W – 3000 kg   L – 8930 mm   D – 650 mm

Platforms   **Flight trajectory**

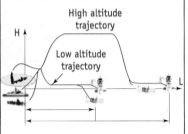

▲   **Fig. 6.9   *BRAHMOS Supersonic Cruise Missile***

countries who denied technology to India that "**We can do it**". Therefore, we see that technology denials and control regimes did not have the impact on aerospace programmes as envisaged by other countries. Technology denied is, in India's case, technology gained.

> *Technology denied is technology gained.*

AEROSPACE PROFILE FOR 2020

Looking ahead, with core competency established in aerospace systems and with large talented manpower available, we will see LCA reigning the skies with air-to-air missile ASTRA and SU 30 MKI with indigenous avionics, launching BRAHMOS missile as its weapon, NAL flight testing SARAS and DRDO embarking on advanced UAV's with weapon delivery capabilities (Fig. 6.10). We will also see ISRO launching advanced GSLVs and PSLVs with heavier satellites and focusing their attention on the moon mission.

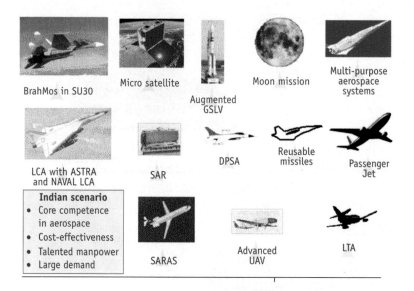

BrahMos in SU30

Micro satellite

Augmented
GSLV

Moon mission

Multi-purpose
aerospace
systems

LCA with ASTRA
and NAVAL LCA

SAR

DPSA

Reusable
missiles

Passenger
Jet

Indian scenario
- Core competence
  in aerospace
- Cost-effectiveness
- Talented manpower
- Large demand

SARAS

Advanced
UAV

LTA

▲ **Fig. 6.10 *Aerospace India: Possible Profile for 2020***

ISRO has commenced a programme for developing micro satellites with the academy participation. Looking beyond, one can see the use of hypersonic reusable missiles, Indian-made passenger jets, and possibly the first version of the hyperplane. The hyperplane is a masterpiece for achieving higher payload efficiency; this Indian concept of 'mass addition' in space has been acknowledged by the world experts, as realisable. The world will also soon see countries utilising biotechnology in space missions and designing blended wing aircraft, which can transport thousands of people in a single flight. Other critical technologies will include secure communication systems and high-power microwave and laser, multi-sensor data fusion, and so on.

The world will also soon see countries utilising biotechnology in space missions and designing blended wing aircraft, which can transport thousands of people in a single flight.

Passenger Aircraft

A study undertaken by the committee of experts on India's Vision 2020 has indicated a large potential for aircraft production in India. The Technology Vision 2020 has estimated that the Indian market holds a demand for fifty six 300-seater aircraft, thirty one 200-seater aircraft, seventy 150-seater aircraft, and sixty five 100-seater aircraft. Similarly in the export market, there is demand of about two hundred eighty 100-seater aircraft. From the findings, it has been concluded that it will be economically viable to produce a 120-seater aircraft in India (Fig. 6.11).

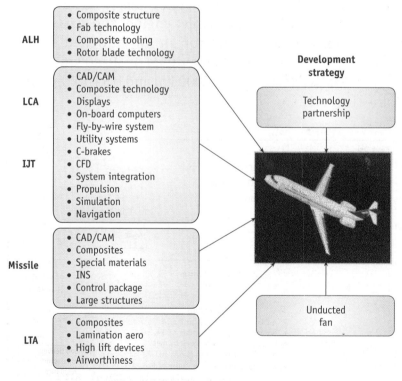

▲ **Fig. 6.11** *120-Seater Passenger Aircraft*

The technology developed through LCA, ALH, IJT and missiles on the composite structure, break pads, fly-by-wire control system, inertial navigation system, control packages, and special materials are available within the country. What is needed, is to integrate these technologies with light transport aircraft, which is being jointly developed by India and Russia through technology partnership between aerospace industries and academic institutions and develop the 120-seater passenger aircraft. The studies have also shown potential for large fuel efficiency by using unducted fans.

Hypersonic Reusable Vehicles

Hypersonic technology is an emerging area to achieve greater speeds using Ramjet and Scramjet engine, and reusability. A study has been carried out for an air-launched reusable hypersonic missile flying at an altitude of 30–40 km in cruise mode at Mach 7 to a range of 2000 km and back to the launch point (Fig. 6.12).

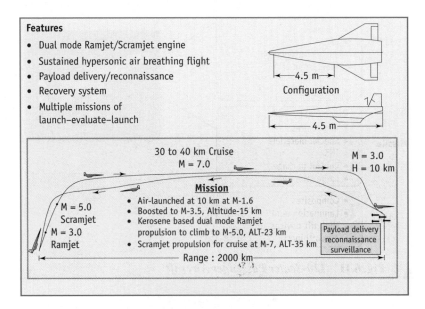

▲   **Fig. 6.12** *Hypersonic Reusable Missile*

Such missions will be highly useful for multiple applications. In the case of the hyperplane, the aim was to achieve larger payload fraction. The space shuttle of USA with 2000 tonnes take-off weight could launch only 30 tonnes in low earth orbit, giving a payload fraction of 1.5% (Figure 6.13). India's concept of the hyperplane aims to realise

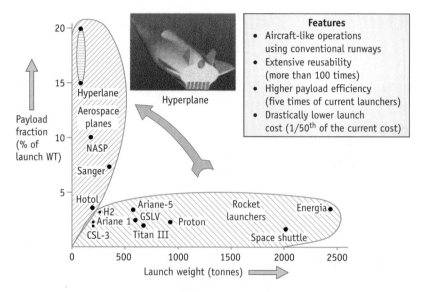

Fig. 6.13 *Payload Effectiveness of Aerospace Vehicles*

15% of payload fraction. This will considerably reduce the launch cost per mission and will enable multiple missions such as transport, reconnaissance, payload delivery, satellite injection, etc. A typical mission of the hyperplane (Figure 6.14) takes off with 100 tonnes weight using fan Ramjet engine, works on Scramjet mode for nearly 1000 sec, during which time it collects the leftover air, cools it, and separates as liquid oxygen. This increases its weight to 166 tonnes; thereafter it flies in rocket engine mode using the liquid oxygen and stored liquid hydrogen to deliver a payload of 15–16 tonnes. This unique concept of mass addition in flight has been conceived by Indian scientists and patented.

Design challenges in hypersonic technologies are given in Figure 6.15. Pioneering efforts have been undertaken in India to demonstrate Scramjet propulsion technology and efforts are on experimenting with air liquefaction.

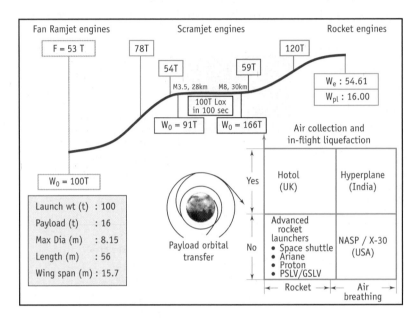

▲   **Fig. 6.14**   *Hyperplane Mission Profile*

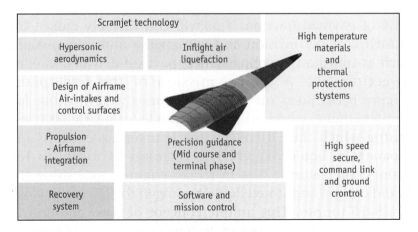

▲   **Fig. 6.15**   *Hypersonic Technology Design Challenges*

Reusable Launch Vehicles and Cost Effective Strategies

India is a country, which has tremendous capabilities in information and communication technology. This combined with space technology will provide greater opportunities for India to be one among the lead countries for future space activities. Therefore, it is an opportune moment for countries to join together with India and launch major universal missions and share the benefit of space to the whole mankind, rather than commercial competition. This will enable narrowing the difference between developing and developed nations.

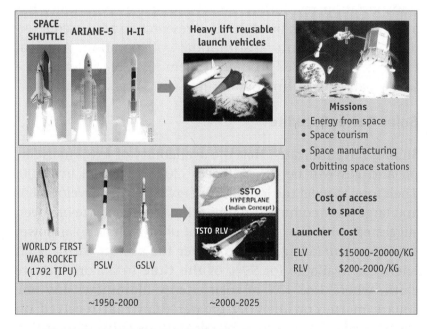

Fig. 6.16 *Cost Reduction Strategies for Reusable Launch Vehicles*

The key to new opportunities for the global space community lies in the creation of new markets arising from mankind's determination to reduce the Man-Planet conflict and embark on solutions for facing the impending crisis for energy, water and mineral resources. Cost reduction strategies for reusable launch vehicles are given in Fig. 6.16.

Formulating of such new missions would thus lead to better capacity utilization, and the creation of low-cost space transportation. India is already working to evolve innovative design concepts for both small as well as large payloads into space. Both single and two-stage reusable launch vehicle concepts are being examined. The goal here is to reduce the cost of access to space by one and two orders of magnitude. Even a small scientific breakthrough, for example, in air-breathing propulsion systems may lead to a space transportation revolution. The world space community has a huge stake in such breakthrough research in advanced inter-disciplinary and inter-institutional collaboration. A global effort is thus needed to quickly demonstrate, at least on a small-scale, the technology for low-cost access to space.

Solar Power Satellite

Studies have indicated that the availability of fossil fuels like oil and gas will be exhausted by 2075 and coal by 2100. Therefore, to meet the looming energy crisis, the development and large-scale commercial utilisation of outer space has been suggested, with the construction of photovoltaic solar power satellites generating electric power for use on earth. Solar energy is available for 99% of the time in an orbit above earth, where 1.43 KW of solar energy illuminates any one square metre considerably greater than that received on earth's surface. Large solar power stations convert solar flux into microwave energy and beam it down to receiving stations at off-shore locations on earth (Fig. 6.17). However, the construction of Solar Power Station (SPS) in space would

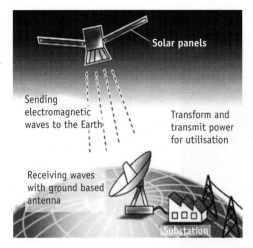

Weight : 10000 metric tonne
Cost : Rs. 450 billion
Area of collector : 12 sq. km
Power on earth : 1000 MW

▲ **Fig. 6.17** *Solar Power Satellite*

necessitate the use of hyperplane, a heavy lift high efficiency space cargo vehicle, using advanced aerospace technologies. Studies have estimated that one SPS generating about 1000 MW would require 12 sq. km array of photovoltaic cells and would weigh 10000 tonnes. Such SPS would take about 3 years for construction in space using a fleet of hyperplanes to place construction materials in low earth orbit.

Space Colony

With the world population topping 6 billion people and expected to reach over 30 billion within the next 100 years, efforts are being made to explore the possibility of accommodating people and building a city in space which could house several thousand inhabitants and boast of an environment identical to Earth. The colony will have air and water, lakes and mountains. It will have an artificial gravity and similar atmospheric structure, air-pressure and temperature as existing on earth and people will be able to stand and walk around exactly as they would do on earth. Light would be provided by a massive reflective mirror that would shine the sunrays into the colony. The living quarters would be a donut-shaped (Fig. 6.18). The colony would also

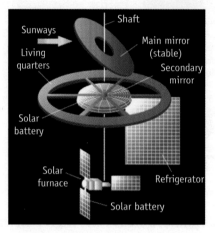

Weight	: 10 million tonne
Cost	: Rs. 12,500 billion
Time	: 20 years

▲ **Fig. 6.18** *Space Colony*

contain areas for agriculture, animals and plants and would weigh about 10 million tonnes. The estimated cost would be approximately Rs. 12,500 billion and would take 20 years to construct the colony.

Prof. Gerard K. O'Neil of Princeton University had visualised the space colony in the earth-moon liberation point and had suggested the launch of so called "space plants". Using a series of Heavy Lift Launch Vehicles (HLLVs) or hyperplanes each carrying hundreds of tonnes of cargos to low earth orbit and assemble and transport these equipments meant for space colony to GEO by a ferry service called space tug. There are two possibilities, one directly taking payloads to space colony from LEO and the other routes is to establish a minimum facility at moon for material mining and reaching the L4/L5 point through catch point L2. This is because if the space colony is to be built at a L4/L5 point between the earth and moon it is thought better to transport the necessary building materials from the moon, since the lunar gravity is 1/6th that of earth and rockets taking off from there would require less fuel. Because of this factor, a factory would need to be set up on the moon before work on the space colony could begin. Materials from the moon can be carried to the colony through lunar materials transfer vehicle. Under this plan, rocks and sand would be gathered on moon and carried to the construction site (Fig. 6.19).

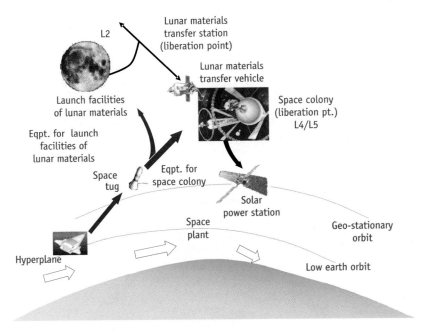

▲   **Fig. 6.19**   *Space Colony at Liberation Point*

Industry Partnership

R&D organisations in India especially ISRO and DRDO have already established partnership with a number of public and private sectors including medium and small-scale industries. SLV-3 and *Prithvi* are outstanding examples to pioneer the large-scale academy and industry participation for technology development and manufacturing. Many Indian industries have graduated over a period of time to become system designers to undertake development and manufacturing of systems, as turnkey projects.

There are more than 300000 engineers and technicians with infrastructure of more than Rs. 10,000 crore in aerospace sector. There is strong mission management culture and committed partnership. With this national strength and opportunity for large demand in aerospace systems and export potential, a large business for industries is knocking at our doors. It is essential that this strength is integrated into an Aerospace Industry Complex for realising high performance cost effective aerospace systems and to make India as one of the leading aerospace countries in the futuristic aerospace missions. Industry development is vital for exports which will lead to higher GDP and economic prosperity.

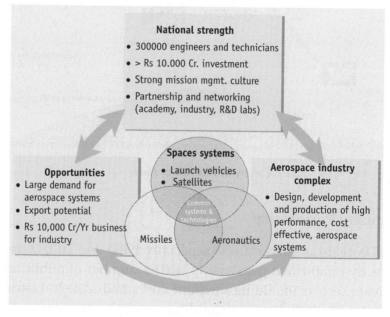

▲   **Fig. 6.20   *Aerospace Technology Integrated Strength***

Combating Failures

High Technology strategic projects in India had its share of failures, but the seeds of success were sown due to these failures. In aerospace projects, after years of development and effort by many scientists, technicians, industries and institutions, a system gets proved through flight trials. Failures in such flight trials in the area of aerospace are common. Of course,

In fact, failures are to be faced courageously so that the teams focus on evaluating the design and results critically.

the mission and project teams get discouraged but the technical experts who review such failures get immense knowledge. In fact, failures occurring in the initial part of the project give excellent results and lead to building up the team.

There are few cases which we ourselves experienced. On August 10, 1979 the first experimental launch of SLV-3 failed to achieve its mission objective of injecting Rohini Satellite in low-earth orbit. Seven years of continuous effort to develop SLV-3, culminated into the mission failure which demoralised the scientists and technologists. With the strong leadership of Prof. Satish Dhawan, the team started to identify the reasons and took corrective actions. The launch on July 18, 1980 (SLV-3 E02) was a total success.

Similarly during the development of *Prithvi* missile among many successes, P08 (the 8th flight of Prithvi missile) was a failure. A Failure Analysis Board, with experts, identified the reasons, evolved experiments to implement solutions and verified in simulation, the performance of the mission before launch. There were similar experiences in *Agni*, ASLV and PSLV.

Failures should not deter the projects. In fact, failures are to be faced courageously so that the teams focus on evaluating the design and results critically. The fruit of the immense experience on analysing failures should not be overlooked. But there should be a strategy for recovery with the full support of top leaders. A good leadership owns the responsibility of failures and makes the project team free from hassles. The same leadership provides adequate support to the project leadership to characterise the failure and find solutions using experts available in the country. PSLV, *Agni*, *Prithvi* are operational after many successful tests.

CONCLUDING REMARKS

In the coming decade, five major technological revolutions will be taking place the world over in the strategic sector.

- Integration of multiple technologies of supersonic aircraft, missiles, and spacecraft to transform into unmanned stealth supersonic long range and low radar cross-section aircraft. This may replace manned fighter aircraft.

- High precision supersonic cruise missiles will replace the current generation of subsonic cruise missiles. These fast and low radar cross-section missiles will be difficult to detect and will give very short reaction time for the enemy's defences.

- Anti-ballistic missile with its satellite network, to protect land and airspace, will become an integral part of the national defence. This will have capability to destroy nuclear weapons.

- Cyber warfare (info-war) will dominate the future war with adversaries trying to breaking into each other computer network to gain control of the vital resources. Information Warfare will become more lethal. India can take the initiatives through its core competence of Information Technology, for gaining the advantage.

- Design and development of hyperplane—a reusable and cost effective launch vehicle for multi-missions. This mission calls for multinational partnership.

The above five significant systems in the strategic sector have more influence in the ICT—which also has influence in the knowledge economy.

7

Integrated Knowledge Economy

INTRODUCTION

Twenty first century belongs to the knowledge age, where acquisition, possession and application of knowledge is the most important resource. Therefore, it is necessary for developing countries like India to mature into a knowledge society and to examine the ways and means by which they can transform themselves into a knowledge economy. The chapter examines this aspect in detail. The chapter also presents innovative models specific to India, like initiatives for bringing in transparency in government administration and management.

Prof. Kalam discussing with the students on their innovative ideas

" In the 21ˢᵗ Century, knowledge is the primary production resource, instead of capital or labour **"**

KNOWLEDGE SOCIETY—DEFINITION AND CHARACTERISTICS

Knowledge society, according to Peter F Drucker, is defined as a society which has the following.

(i) Borderlessness, because knowledge travels even more effortlessly than money.

(ii) Upward mobility, available to every one through easily acquired formal education.

(iii) The potential for failure as well as success. Anyone can acquire the "means of production", i.e., the knowledge required for the job, but not everyone can win.

The twenty first century belongs to the knowledge society. Therefore, nations will build themselves into knowledge societies by understanding the dynamics of knowledge and transforming it into wealth.

Knowledge society has the following distinct characteristics:

(i) It uses knowledge through all its constituents and endeavours, to empower and enrich its people.

(ii) It uses knowledge as a powerful tool to drive societal transformation.

(iii) It is a learning society committed to innovation.

(iv) It has the capacity to generate, absorb, disseminate and protect knowledge and also use it to create economic wealth and social good for all its constituents.

Societal Transformation

During the last few centuries, the world has undergone several social transformations. It started as an agricultural society where manual labour was the key factor and the economic growth was dependent largely on natural products such as raw materials as well as agricultural products.

With the advent of industrial revolution, economic progress was propelled largely by technological development leading to machines, replacing human resources.

India could not fully reap the results of the Industrial Revolution as the nation was ruled by foreign powers during those decades. However, licensed industrial institutions did emerge.

This society added value to its products through explicit knowledge, which is technology, to produce industrial products that led to the economic growth of nations. Thus management of technology, capital, and labour provided the competitive advantage to bring about this transformation in economic growth.

The world has already moved into an information society. This society derives its economic growth by further value addition to the explicit knowledge through networking. Connectivity and software products are now driving the economies of the nations in this society. Figure 1.7 (Chapter 1) discussed the details.

Tomorrow's world would be one which would recognise knowledge in its most comprehensive form and add further value to the products through innovative knowledge-intensive products/services in a networked ambience. These knowledge products would largely contribute to the economic growth of nations.

The precious assets of a country are the skill, ingenuity, imagination, and civilisational strength of its people. With globalisation triggering competition, the key distinguishing feature will be the ability of people, in different countries, to invoke and use these native strengths to their full advantage and provide the much-needed competitive edge. This, subjective knowledge, heuristics, imagination, and all those attitudes that make us human, should be integrated for laying the foundation for enunciating plans corresponding to their requirements and competency. This knowledge, with further learning and training in skills, would provide the quintessential intrinsic strength to be competitive. This would be the key for economic growth and national strength now and well into the future.

In the 21st century, knowledge is the primary production resource, instead of capital or labour. Efficient utilisation of this existing knowledge can create comprehensive wealth for the nation in the form of better health, education, infrastructure, and other social indicators. The ability to create and maintain the knowledge infrastructure, develop knowledge workers and enhance their productivity through creation, nurturing and exploitation of new knowledge will be the key factors in deciding the prosperity of the knowledge society. Such a knowledge society has two very important components: societal transformation and wealth generation. Let us discuss how India can transform itself into a full-fledged knowledge society and thereafter into an integrated knowledge economy within a decade by leveraging its unique competencies.

KNOWLEDGE TRADITION OF INDIA

As we discussed earlier, India is a country richly endowed with natural resources and with 1 billion people as its precious human resource. In addition, the country enjoys competitive advantages in certain areas. Let us look at the broad spectrum of these assets that we have and the connected issues.

A view of the impressive achievements of the Indian civilisation reinforces the belief that India was an advanced society in the millennia gone by. There was a continual process of intellectual renaissance through inspiring contributions by saints of many faiths, philosophers, poets, scientists, astronomers, and mathematicians. Their new and original thoughts, principles, and practices provided a solid foundation to our own knowledge society.

In the field of education, it is an acknowledged fact that great universities such as Takshashila and Nalanda existed, where students not only from India, but also from such far off places like Babylon, Greece, Syria, Arabia, and China came to study diverse subjects—language, grammar, philosophy, medicine, surgery, archery, accounts, commerce, futurology, documentation, occult, music, dance, and the art of discovering hidden treasures. The panel of masters included renowned names, such as Kautilya, Panini, Jivak, Abhinav Gupta, and Patanjali.

> *India invented the dynamic number zero, which laid the foundation of the binary system of counting that present-day computers depend upon.*

India invented the dynamic number zero, which laid the foundation of the binary system of counting that present-day computers depend upon. **Albert Einsten said, "We owe it to the Indians, who taught us how to count, without which no worthwhile scientific discovery could have been made."** Similarly, it was India that originated the decimal system.

Much before Euclid, geometry was used in India as '*Gyaamiti*'. Aryabhatta defined *Pi* as the ratio of circumference to the diameter of a circle and worked out its value to four decimals.

Similarly, 1500 years ago, Bhaskaracharya in '*Surya Siddhanta*' calculated the time taken by the earth to orbit the sun to 9 decimal places. Likewise, 1000 years before

Copernicus, Aryabhatta stated that the earth revolves around the sun in his famous *'Aryabhateeam'* while Bhaskaracharya in *'Surya Siddhanta'* discovered the law of gravity. In the field of medicine, Charaka consolidated the Ayurveda and more than 2500 years ago Sushruta conducted complicated surgeries.

We should be proud of our scientific achievements. But all this knowledge is not known to the world outside India, because it has not been researched further or disseminated.

It is not that outstanding achievements are confined to only our ancient past. Before India's independence, we had world class scientists, poets, philosophers, engineers, doctors, and in fact people in almost every profession one could think of. Scientists like S N Bose, Meghnad Saha, J C Bose, Sir C V Raman, Sir K S Krishnan, Homi Bhabha, Vikram Sarabhai, B C Roy; mathematicians like Ramanujam; poets like Rabindranath Tagore, philosopher saints like Vivekananda. The post-Independence Era too has witnessed equally great achievements.

Post-independence India launched its first Five Year Plan. This led to the establishment of important industries and building of infrastructure. The 1970s saw the results of the First Green Revolution leading to self-sufficiency in food. Operation Flood led to India becoming the highest producer of milk in due course of time. Science and technology also witnessed a major push and brought about the formation of many R&D and S&T institutions, spearheaded by eminent leaders from various fields. This led to a scientific temper and a firm foundation for high technology missions.

The firm foundation laid by India's satellite and satellite launch vehicle programmes has given the country the capability to indigenously design and develop any type of satellite and launch it into orbit from its own soil through its own launch vehicles. The recent seventh successive successful flight of Polar Satellite Launch Vehicle (PSLV C-5) injecting RESOURCE SAT-1 in sun synchronous orbit demonstrated India's might in indigenous capability. Similarly, India is also capable of designing, developing, and producing any type of missile or warhead. Induction of *Prithvi* and *Agni* by the Indian Army is a testimony of this indigenous capability. Our achievements in the area of nuclear power generation and weapon development are at par with those of the developed world.

> *It is time, India captures this unique opportunity to transform itself into a knowledge power and eventually transform itself into a developed country.*

Indian software is performing well in the international business market. Large pools of young entrepreneurs are responsible for such a change. Our skilled human resource is one of the most sought-after resource in the world. This is evident from the major contribution of the Indian scientists and entrepreneurs to the economic growth of the developed world. In addition, India is uniquely placed to quickly raise a huge pool of knowledge workers, which very few developed nations are capable of, in view of its population and availability of educated manpower.

India has certain assets and advantages that few nations of the world can proudly claim. We must recognise our glorious past and our present contributions and competitive advantages to chalk out our future. The world is moving over to a knowledge society where networked knowledge would be the currency of power and wealth. It is time India captures this unique opportunity to transform itself into a knowledge power and eventually transform itself into a developed country within the next two decades. To bring about this transformation, it is essential to know where we stand with respect to competitiveness, which is the real engine for transition to a knowledge power.

COMPETITIVENESS—THE DRIVING FORCE

The indices of world competitiveness are based on the global competitiveness report prepared by the World Economic Forum. The Forum has defined competitiveness as 'the ability of a national economy to achieve sustained high rates of economic growth'. As per this definition, the ranking of different countries as of 2002–2003 are:

USA [1], Taiwan [3], Singapore [4], Australia [7], Hong Kong [17], China [33], India [48].

Global competitiveness is decided by a triangular combination consisting of progressiveness of industry, technology, and status of governmental deregulation, all working in unison.

Technology-led industrial growth can be sustained only through establishing an innovation system. It is through the process of innovation that knowledge is converted into wealth. The characteristics of knowledge economics are given in Fig. 7.1. Further, innovation is an important factor for the competitiveness of both service and manufacturing sectors and hence the urgent need to put in place an innovation system. Such a system would involve a network of firms, knowledge-producing institutions, bridging institution, and customers/users in a value addition—creating production chain (Fig. 7.2). With such a consortium, the innovation system would tap into the growing stock of global knowledge, assimilate and adapt it to local needs and finally create new knowledge and technology. India must evolve such systems to improve its competitiveness in the global marketplace.

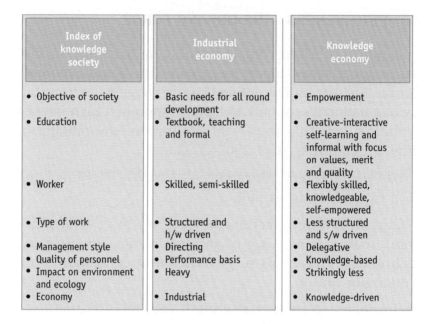

Fig. 7.1   Characteristics of Knowledge Economics

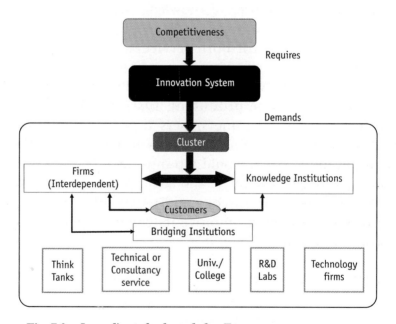

Fig. 7.2   Ingredients for knowledge Economy

Competitiveness emerges from the strength of knowledge power, which is powered by technology, which in turn, is powered by capital. As discussed earlier, in the agrarian society, competitiveness emerged from human power. In the case of an industrial society, competitiveness came exclusively from technology, manufacturing equipment, and tools. In an information society, competitiveness comes through the ability to collaborate and network resources and competencies across the world. In the coming knowledge society, competitiveness would be derived from the ability to recognise and integrate all forms of knowledge leading to innovation in every area of human endeavour.

POWER OF KNOWLEDGE—INTEGRATED STRENGTH

We would like to share with you the importance of knowledge and how integrated knowledge and decision-making processes can lead to competitiveness and help, meet challenges.

(a) Software Solution for Improving the Hardware System

During the development of one of the missile systems, we wanted to realise a very accurate guidance and control, to ensure better accuracy for the missile to reach its target. This can be realised, only if we have highly accurate gyro sensors. The specification demanded a gyro with a drift of less than 0.1 degree per hour. But the gyros produced in India by our industry had a drift of one degree per hour. There was denial of sale of high accuracy sensors from developed countries in the name of MTCR (Missile Technology Control Regime). A task team was, therefore, formed with members drawn from a University and three R&D labs to find the technical solution of using software to improve the accuracy of the gyro. About

12 young software and hardware engineers worked nearly eight months and came up with a unique solution. They suggested that a fast algorithm could be loaded on the on-board computer of the missile, after conducting extensive design, system engineering and simulation efforts, including verifying the integrated software and hardware through hardware-in-loop-simulation and trajectory analysis.

This software could predict the error ahead of the flight on real time. While the missile is flying, it could analyse the present state, apply drift compensation and effect control force corrections. A better accuracy in the hardware had been achieved with the introduction of innovative software and system engineering. And resulted in achieving one of the best guidance and control system. The Indian Army has inducted this missile system. Young minds proved to very powerful, when challenges were put before them.

(b) Control Law for LCA

Another classic example, is the concept of integrating knowledge spread in multiple institutions through a National Team for the development of Control Law of the Light Combat Aircraft, now called *Tejas*. The LCA management wanted to develop control law for LCA indigenously, as no country was parting with the technology. The status of existing competencies in various work centres in the country to undertake the design, the availability of software and hardware engineers and the views of experts were considered. They realised that the capabilities were spread out in various institutions, R&D laboratories and the industry. It was decided to form a national team, integrating the expertise and adding young scientists to the team and for defining the missions for the development of control law on a fast track. The team took up the challenge and successfully completed this work in a record time.

After the May 1998 nuclear test, when India declared itself a nuclear state, the joint development contract for development of LCA flight control system with a firm in the US was abruptly withdrawn. Because of the experience gained by our young control law national team, we could see the confidence in our research laboratories and partners to realise the flight control system for LCA through indigenous effort, with little additional time. We were successful.

The national team concept was also used in the development of Carbon Fibre Composite (CFC) Wings which is the largest composite product ever made in the country with advanced technology process. Here again the National Team, from multiple institutions proved successful. Similarly multiple research laboratories, academy, industry and users joined together through a national team for Flight Test Centre of LCA. This integrated strength brought systematic approach in integration, hardware-in-loop-simulation for evaluation of each sub-system's performance in the integrated set-up, quality assurance, certification and fight testing of LCA. More than 100 flight tests of TD-1 and TD-2 have been successfully carried out. LCA is on its course for induction in the Indian Air Force and will be a candidate in the international market.

Both, certain missile and LCA technologies brought out the best of competitiveness in our scientific and technological community and our ability to work in a networked ambience. We would like to assert that India has the competitive edge in realising any high technology system, provided the challenges are well defined and the young people are brought together as integrated teams with mission definition to achieve the results, in a time bound manner. We have to bring out our latent excellence by breaking narrow departmental constraints and work as integrated teams through mission mode programmes.

KNOWLEDGE EMPOWERED SOCIETY

Knowledge has also been a driver for social development. A society, which has capacity to create, absorb, disseminate, protect and use knowledge, can create economic wealth and societal transformation. And the societal transformation will occur through the development of education, healthcare, agriculture and governance.

These, in turn, will lead to generation of employment, high productivity, and rural prosperity. Recognising this potential, the Planning Commission of India formed a task force to evolve action plans for transforming India into a knowledge power (Fig. 7.3). This team has identified wealth generation as a very important task for the nation, which has to be woven around national competencies. The task team has also identified the following core areas that will spearhead our march towards a knowledge society: Information and communication technology (ICT), biotechnology, weather forecasting, disaster management, telemedicine and tele-education, technologies to produce native knowledge products, service sector, and infotainment (an emerging area resulting from the convergence of information and entertainment). These core technologies, fortunately, can be interwoven by IT.

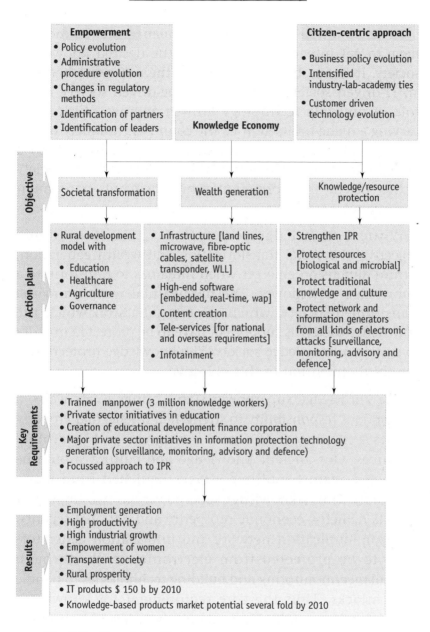

Fig. 7.3 Knowledge Economy

Hence, multiple technologies and management structures have to get integrated to generate the desired knowledge society. It has to be recognised that the difference between an IT-driven society and a knowledge-driven society is the role of multiple technology growth engines. With India carving a niche for itself in IT, the country is uniquely placed to capitalise on the opportunity to transform into a knowledge society. The foundation for a knowledge society is the societal transformation, which demands transparent governance.

While a knowledge society has a two-dimensional objective of societal transformation and wealth generation, a third dimension emerges when India has to transform to a knowledge superpower. The hard-earned wealth and the transformed society, which are two pillars on which the knowledge society is supported, have to be protected in order to sustain a knowledge society. The knowledge protection is the third dimension of this objective.

The knowledge superpower status brings in its wake, a tremendous responsibility to strengthen Intellectual Property Rights and protect the vast biological and microbial resources. Our ancient knowledge and culture should be protected against multiple attacks launched from many directions. Thus a knowledge superpower has two important aspects namely—economic prosperity and national security. Our communication network and information generators have to be protected from electronic attacks through surveillance/monitoring and building technologies to handle such attacks. Thus the core requirement for knowledge protection is two-fold. There should be a focused approach to Intellectual Property Rights and related issues and major private sector initiatives have to be launched in the area of technology generation for information security.

KNOWLEDGE MANAGEMENT IN GOVERNANCE

One of the challenges for anyone who deals with government agencies, is its sheer complexity. There is now an increasing awareness in the central and state governments to bring in functional agencies that could facilitate one-stop shops for all the needs of the citizens. Persons in this one-stop shops may themselves have to do much coordination within the complex systems. Modern IT tools help accelerate such coordination. Eventually, it can reach real-time capability as has been achieved for railway reservations.

However such an operational system is yet to emerge in many other areas of government: banking, tax or electricity bill payment, etc. Actions by some of the state/central government departments have resulted in the launch of comprehensive and user-friendly Internet portals. Portals of this nature are being attempted only in some states like Andhra Pradesh, Tamil Nadu, Karnataka, and Madhya Pradesh. In these states, electronic network systems are being used to provide market-related information, land records, and foodstock records. But these actions are in an initial introductory phase. In one state, a florist participates in a flower auction in the Netherlands, using real-time communication.

With this background, it is essential that government functions, which have interfaces or interactions with public (especially where the state and central functionaries have to serve or support or even correct the citizens) should be done through the tools of ICT. Software has to be written to codify the rules, procedures, and other related government functions and public access should be through IT with the necessary access control to govern in a transparent manner. Since India has the core competence in ICT, success in bringing in transparency in administration and management through e-commerce and e-business leading to e-governance is definitely possible. Actions have to be initiated in a mission mode. Appropriate legal instruments must be formulated to empower governments for such modes of interactions. These developments are contingent upon the establishment of electronic connectivity in both rural and urban areas.

Knowledge Society can be developed by adopting appropriate strategies for knowledge creation (e.g., improvements in education, training of human resources, preserving knowledge through IPR, etc.) and by adopting strategies for exploiting knowledge through the acquisition of technology, development of infrastructure (including IT) and promoting venture capital. The core strength and the development pattern vary from country to country. Depending on the situation, the type of training/education and infrastructure required to sustain the knowledge society has to be decided.

Since knowledge of all types will be the engine of growth in a knowledge society, it becomes necessary to manage this knowledge at the national level. A nationwide knowledge management framework is suggested in Fig. 7.4. Nationwide knowledge management involves setting up of infrastructure, processes, policies and practices which will lead to an environment where knowledge creation is encouraged, nurtured, rewarded and finally exploited for achieving the nation's economy and social objectives.

A nation's S&T, fiscal, trade and industrial policies need to be evolved based on the nation's strength's, weaknesses, environmental threats and opportunities. The strategies involved in knowledge creation, knowledge exploitation and knowledge infrastructure finally lead to wealth generation and improvement in national economic indicators. The strategies are:

  (i) Preserving knowledge through IPR

 (ii) R&D through knowledge networks

(iii) Human resource planning and development

(iv) Promoting venture capital

 (v) National and international market development

(vi) Selected technology acquisitions, and

(vii) Infrastructure development.

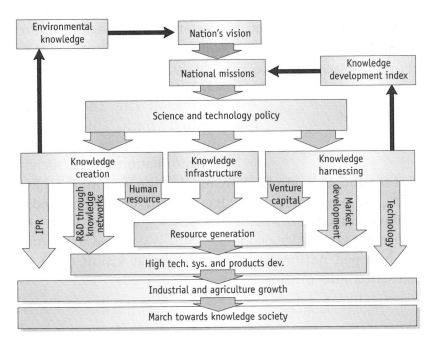

▲ **Fig. 7.4** *Framework for Nationwide Knowledge Management*

Assessing the extent of development in a knowledge society requires the development of an index, which can be called the Knowledge Development Index to measure the extent of development in terms of knowledge creation, absorption, dissemination, protection and use of knowledge. For example, creation of knowledge can be measured in terms of the number of research papers published, dissemination can be linked to the density of newspapers, etc. Such an index, besides providing information, would also provide a feedback for introducing necessary correctives.

CONCLUDING REMARKS

"When learning is purposeful, creativity blossoms;

when the creativity blossoms, thinking emanates;

when thinking emanates, knowledge is fully lit;

when knowledge is lit, economy flourishes".

As the world transforms into a knowledge society, India has a tremendous advantage to become a knowledge economy, due to its core competence in certain technologies including IT, vast natural resources and above all the 300 million ignited youth. This strength must be harnessed fully for the transformation of the society and for the generation of wealth for the nation. We have seen, the power of knowledge and the competitive edge achieved in certain mission mode programmes. With the integrated knowledge economy, India is destined to become a developed nation by 2020. This great vision must be translated into missions.

Vision to Mission

8

INTRODUCTION

So far, we have discussed four major mission areas such as agriculture, healthcare, manufacturing and strategic sector and also knowledge based economy. This chapter brings out missions in education, water, energy, rural development and others, which are essential to be undertaken for the forward movement of economic development and prosperity of the nation. Above all, for achieving the missions the essential requirement is creative leadership.

Dr. Kalam presenting Developed India Vision to Parliamentarians

> **❝** Invisible leadership is exercising the vision to change
> the traditional role
> from commander to coach,
> from manager to mentor,
> from director to delegator, and
> from one who demands respect to one who
> facilitates self-respect **❞**

THE TRANSFORMATION

The earlier chapters brought out the salient features of the vision of a developed India, and technological advancements in agriculture, manufacturing, healthcare and strategic sectors. Also it highlighted the roadmap for creating a integrated knowledge economy and enabling societal transformation in India using our core competencies in technology and the better utilisation of human and natural resources. We believe that India, with its vast resources and value system, has the potential to be the one amongst the few developed centres in the world. But on the surface there are problems which make it appear as if the nation is chaotic. India will, however, emerge as a strong nation both in the economic front and security, with little correction but optimum utilisation of our valuable resources. Also mission mode programmes and an effective management structure will facilitate this transition.

The world is going through a major technological transformation and a continuous updation of knowledge. This revolution will go on, whether we participate or not. Therefore, it is essential that we must take advantage of the technological revolution, which can make our country a developed nation in the years to come. The 'technology edge' is possible only if India launches high technology research and learning in academic institutions and integrates our R&D

Labs, with the industries to make high technology products, which will be competitive in the world market. In order to become an economic power, India must get a sizable global market share for high technology systems and products.

Our own attitude will be the key to the future. The most important thing is that every Indian must know that India is rich in resources. Therefore, it is essential, that with hope we change our attitude to progress, follow the optimistic route and create a movement among the youth to transform India into a developed country. The power within comes with a degree of responsibility. We individually hold the future in our hands. Perhaps the most important requirement is the acceptance that we are living in a great country, and as the inheritors of the great civilisation and the largest democracy in the world, India deserves the right place on this planet. We trust every Indian will accept this view point. Any pessimistic view will push us towards the dark age. One should not forget the sacrifices of our great leaders for freedom. Therefore, all of us must resolve to work for those missions that will lead the nation to prosperity, peace, happiness and security.

CONVERGENCE OF TECHNOLOGY

Knowledge in the form of information technology has thrown up the opportunity for India to become a premier supplier of computer software and IT enabled services to the industrial world. IT has not only provided increased employment but also revolutionised the pattern of work in all spheres of the economy by promoting speed, transparency, quality and efficiency. It has also transformed the way we communicate within the country and with the rest of the world, shrinking distance. The information technology and communication technology have already converged, leading to ICT. Now, nanotechnology is knocking at our doors. This will replace micro-electro mechanical systems and many other areas with their potential application in the field of medicine, electronics and material sciences. When nanotechnology and ICT meet, an integrated silicon electronics and photonics will be born. When biotechnology is integrated with ICT, bioinformatics is born. When ICT, nanotechnology, integrated silicon electronics and photonics and sensors converge, intelligent systems will emerge. When all the above get integrated, knowledge powered superior human being is born.

MISSIONS FOR THE VISION

During the interaction with a large population from all walks of life across the country, whether it is a remote village in Kerala or a far away rural state in Nagaland or Uri in J&K, the area close to the line of control, we felt the aspiration for living in a prosperous India and making our country developed within the next two decades. Therefore, the time has already come to get on with the defined missions with the identified chief executives for each of the missions and appropriate management structure and funding.

EDUCATION

Literacy Movement

In ancient times, India was a great centre for learning. Scholars from 30 countries studied *vedas*, logic, grammar, religious philosophy, astronomy, medicine and mathematics at the Nalanda University. Sadly, today India does not enjoy that glory in the field of education.

Our literacy rate is only 65%. India spends 3.8% of its GNP on education. 46% of our population, 15 years and above are illiterates. Several national policies on education have come and gone, but still a major concerted effort is needed to eradicate illiteracy completely. Some of the states have done extremely well, but still much needs to be done. Recently the Education Bill has been enacted for compulsory education up to high school level. This must be implemented. A drive for educating all our children is essential.

We are fortunate to have some of the excellent schools and professional institutes like IICs, IITs and IIMs. As we transform into a knowledge society, it is essential that education must occupy the highest place. The vast resource of 700 million below the age of 35 years can be used for making a prosperous economy. But at the same time, the cost of education and affordability by lower income group must be ensured, with quality education.

Women Education

There must be upmost priority for women education. When the women are empowered, a stable society will emerge. It will result in a small family and a better education to the children. We have to ensure the continuity of secondary education and university education for girls. We must establish e-learning connecting schools and colleges. Education should also provide avenues for vocational training, and transform students into entrepreneurs.

Adult Education

Also a systematic planning to impart education to 100 million illiterate adults must be instituted. During vacations, students and teachers of high schools can undertake teaching adults from nearby villages. Each student must help atleast five adults and enable them to read and write. Parents must encourage such activities of their children.

Quality Teachers

Teachers should be the best minds in the country. Quality teachers by virtue of their intellect and moral leadership, attract students for research and impart good qualities to them. This makes the students useful citizens, with the sole aim of development of the country.

Higher Education and Industrial Participation

Higher education is an important factor in realising the knowledge economy and social transformation. Therefore, higher education must be linked to national development. This is possible by introducing certain measures such as:

(a) Integrating investments in development with investments in education.

(b) Developing selected universities to become power-houses of research.

(c) Forming consortia between new economy industries and select university groups.

(d) Establishing university centres for carrying out policy research.

(e) Encouraging investments from the industry.

(f) Devising mechanisms for joint endeavours among academic institutions.

Information and communication technology can be used to connect the faculty, from any university, to multiple class rooms within and other universities. Probably fibre optic leased line cables or a combination of Satellite line (V-Sat) can be used. Today, technology has advanced to such an extent that we can even think of storing all the human knowledge in digital form. One initiative in this direction is of creating a Universal Digital Library, irrespective of language. In India there is a programme to digitise 250 million pages, say about one million books in two years' time. Modern technologies and machineries are available with us to undertake out this.

REACH Mission

The Department of Science and Technology introduced a mission with 'REACH' (Relevance and Excellence in ACHieving new heights in education institutions). This mission has been launched with the objective of establishing 'Centres of Excellence' in existing engineering institutions

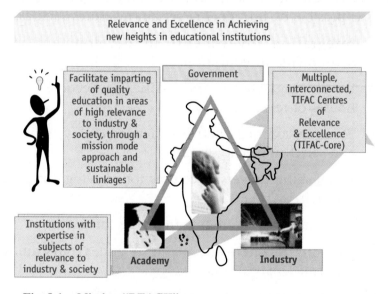

▲   Fig. 8.1   *Mission "REACH"*

to promote areas of industrial relevance and provide the trained manpower to the industries partnering the mission (Fig. 8.1). This is one of the several missions to achieve the vision of Developed India by 2020. The purpose is to establish 80-100 centres, connected electronically, through the faculty exchange, with a common academic programme and joint research, and common perception of the commitment to achieve excellence. Centre(s) Of Relevance and Excellence (CORE) have been established in academic institutions at Dibrugarh, Mumbai, Thanjavur, Madurai, Coimbatore, Surat, etc. in the areas of agro and industrial biotechnology, advanced computing and information processing, clastic petroleum reservoir engineering, industrial safety, environmental engineering, herbal drugs, etc.

In the REACH programme, we experienced the willingness of the industries to participate in specialised areas of their interest and their willingness to invest about 40% of the total expenditure in establishing CORE for which they will receive skilled man-power and research output in specialised areas. It gives us a great confidence that our industries will be partners in mutually beneficial technology development and education initiatives.

> *It gives us a great confidence that our industries will be partners in mutually beneficial technology development and education initiatives.*

WATER MISSION

Today, with a global population of six billion, at least three billion have access to limited or perhaps the abundant supply of water. But by 2025, with world population of 8 billion, it is painful to know that only one billion would have similar access to fresh water. Lack of sanitation which affects two billion people today will affect five billion in the next two decades due to lack of water.

Globally there are a few solutions to this problem of water shortage. However, we have to start now to go far. This can be done by redistribution of water. We have already started this by widespread promotion of rainwater harvesting in both rural and urban areas and also networking of the rivers. In addition to these, we need to put a stop to large scale wastage of water and also impart water recycling technologies to urban and rural areas.

Another regional solution though in the coastal areas, would be to create new, perennial sources of fresh water by sea water desalination. In all these solutions the lead taken by India would become the role model for the other countries. Figure 8.2 indicates the solutions for water for future generations.

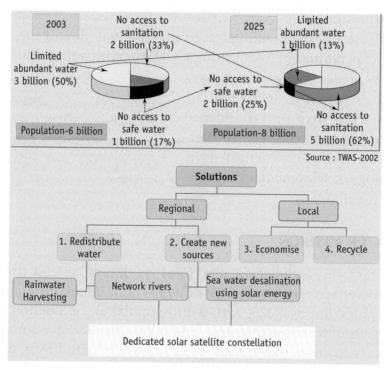

Fig. 8.2   *Water for Future Generations*

Networking of Rivers

Networking of rivers is essential for controlling floods and droughts, for making drinking water available to all regions, for transporting goods and for generating power cultivable land. This mission will also provide employment opportunities to the rural population. And above all, the networking will lead to environmental upgradation and national connectivity.

Science and technology can surely help in executing such mission. Remote sensing can be used for surveying and evolving optimum water routes, for mapping environmental and afforestation requirements, and for continuously monitoring the networked water flow through all seasons and at all times. This will need a dedicated satellite constellation for our networked river systems. It is possible to evolve a scheme by which the 14 Himalayan tributaries of

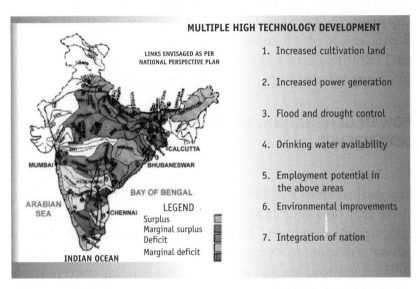

Fig. 8.3   *Challenge for the Young—River Networking*

the Ganges (Fig. 8.3) and Brahmaputra rivers in Northern India can be linked and the same transferred to South via a series of canals and pumping stations across the Vindhya

Mountains to replenish the 17 Southern rivers including the Godavari, Krishna and Cauvery. The task is to be accomplished in a phased manner. The task force set up by the Government is already studying the scheme. Networking of rivers is a challenge for the young.

Space Technology for Water

Seeking new water sources may be yet another thrust area for space science and technology. Reverse osmosis technologies for sea water desalination in a new energy efficient manner, is rapidly evolving. Space-based solar power stations have six to fifteen times greater capital utilisation than equivalent sized ground solar stations. Linking space solar power to reverse osmosis technology for large-scale drinking water supplies to coastal cities is thus yet another major contribution which could be made by space technologies for sustainable economic development through regional solutions for the impending drinking water crisis.

POWER GENERATION, PATTERN OF GLOBAL ENERGY DEPENDENCE

The World Energy Forum has predicted that fossil-based oil and coal reserves will last another 5 to 10 decades. For India, these may be available for a marginally longer period of time. Industrially developed countries use a larger percentage of power generated from nuclear energy. There was a movement in these nations to not add any more nuclear power. These thoughts emanated from many agencies, propagating against electricity generated by nuclear power. Figure 8.4 indicates the pattern of global energy dependence.

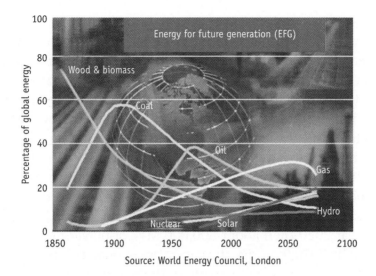

Source: World Energy Council, London

▲ **Fig. 8.4** *Pattern of Global Energy Dependence*

It is important for a nation like ours, which currently generates just 2000–3000 MW, to increase its nuclear power generation capacity to 20,000 MW in 20 years, through the Nuclear Power Corporation. A programme to achieve this target is already in place. India possesses the core competence in this field and the nuclear material, particularly thorium, is abundantly available. India is also getting equipped in the area of nuclear safety, which is of prime importance.

It is important for the youth of India to see the future in a big way and to put forth to the people the scientific view about the importance of nuclear power generation. It can propel the nation towards the generation of nuclear energy and power generated through non-conventional energy sources (like solar, wind, biomass and wave energy), based on India's abundance and the imperative for a clean environment. With this background, the power generation plan in India is discussed in the following paragraphs.

Power generation is one of the important infrastructure sector of the national economy. Its demand has been growing faster than other forms of all energy, at the rate of 7 to 8% and the demand-supply gap has been widened over the years. For the economic development of the country and for providing better quality of life to the people, providing reliable and inexpensive electricity is essential. The installed generating capacity has grown from 1,358 MW in 1947 to 107,973 MW as on March 31, 2003. The growth in demand for power has exceeded the generation capacity in the last 5 decades. If we are to provide quality electric power for all by the year 2020 then about 300,000 MW of power needs to be added by 2020 to bridge the gap between demand and supply. As already discussed in Chapter 6 the potential of generating power from nuclear energy by 2020 is about 20,000 MW, the rest undoubtedly has to be made through other sources like hydro power, thermal, non-conventional energy including wind, wave, biomass and solar power and by using hydrogen. As far as hydro power is concerned, it holds a good promise for bridging the demand gap with its potential in the country estimated about 84,000 MW. The potential from wind energy has been estimated to be of the order to 45,000 MW. The total estimated power from renewable energy source is of the order of 80,000–100,000 MW depending upon the project management. To sum up, by the year 2020, it is possible to generate power of 300,000 MW through nuclear, hydro, thermal, and non-conventional energy sources. In a long term, solar energy from solar power satellite will be the solution.

In order to ensure availability of power to all the sections of the population by 2020, it is essential to reduce transmission and distribution losses in the power sector, as these in India are about 25% compared to the world level of 7–9%. Necessary technology inputs must be used to reduce the loss.

PROVIDING URBAN AMENITIES IN RURAL AREAS (PURA)

India lives in villages, but because of the lack of proper education, employment, healthcare and infrastructure people migrate to cities for a better living. Because of this rush to city, the Indian cities are getting congested without sufficient place for living, and without water and power. The PURA model envisages a habitat designed to improve the quality of life in rural areas and also makes special suggestions to remove urban congestion. Naturally, our most demanding urban problem is that of removal of congestion. Also, efficient supply of water and effective waste disposal in every locality are the paramount civic needs. There is a minimum size below which a habitat is not viable and not competitive within the existing congested city. At the same time, the existing congested city is not economical compared to a new town once the minimum size of expansion is crossed.

As against a conventional city say, rectangular in shape and measuring 10 km by 6 km, the model considers an annular ring-shaped town integrating minimum 10 to 15 villages of the same 60 km sq. area, and the same access distance of 1 km to transport arteries. It needs only one transportation route, half as long as that needed for the rectangular city; so the frequency of transportation will be doubled, halving waiting times. It has zero junctions and will need only a single-level layout. Also, it needs only one route as against eight needed for the rectangular plan, so people will no longer need to change from one line to another to move from any one point to another; that would save communicating time. Further, as all traffic is concentrated into one single route, high-efficiency mass transportation systems become economical, even for a comparatively small population. This cuts costs substantially and is more convenient for the general public.

Knowledge-powered rural development is an essential need for transforming India into a knowledge superpower. High bandwidth rural connectivity is the minimum requirement to take education, healthcare, and economic dynamism to the rural areas.

> *Knowledge-powered rural development is an essential need for transforming India into a knowledge superpower.*

Providing Urban Amenities in Rural Areas (PURA) is essentially conceived around four types of connectivities, with the aim to speed up the process of achieving total rural prosperity.

The first of these connectivities is *Physical Connectivity* — movement of people and goods, access to schools, health centres and markets (Fig. 8.5). In our rural areas today, there are inadequate roads, rail and public infrastructure. With more than 580,000 villages in India, the means to physical connectivity is to organise these villages in clusters, from 10 upwards.

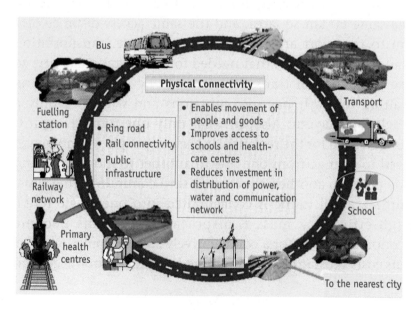

▲   **Fig. 8.5   *PURA—Physical Connectivity***

This cluster of villages needs to be provided physical connectivity by near ring roads. Low cost buses, preferably driven by batteries energised by renewable energy sources, and powered by high efficiency engine would be operated almost throughout the day as shuttle services moving people and goods from village to village and village to school, health centre, fuelling stations, farming areas, warehouses, agro-industries and other commercial centres.

Thus, the heart of the PURA concept is Physical Connectivity of 10 or more villages by a ring road covering a population of around 30,000–50,000 people. Connectivity, thereafter, to a rail network and to a nearest city beyond this village cluster would take off from the ring road. All these roads or links will be of high quality enabling high speed transportation.

This is potentially a cost effective solution for activating the schools, health centres, village markets, warehouses and commercial centres that would serve the population of the entire cluster, thus resulting in economies of scale. Also these clusters will become an excellent investment destination because the transactional costs will be much lower than in the metropolis. In addition, quality of life will be improved.

Similarly PURA needs to be provided with Electronic Connectivity (Fig. 8.6). The system oriented approach for the village cluster would require to introduce teleeducation for farmers and villagers, village internet kiosks, public call offices, telemedicine, e-market, e-governance, e-commerce and so on. Thus, the revolution in Information Technology supported by space-based technology would create the needed societal transformation at the grass-roots of the country. It also will provide the opportunity for the villagers to collectively locate call centres, business processing out-sourcing and software development centres to use outside markets. Thus PURA provides a seamless connection and movement of molecules (people), atoms (material) and electrons (knowledge).

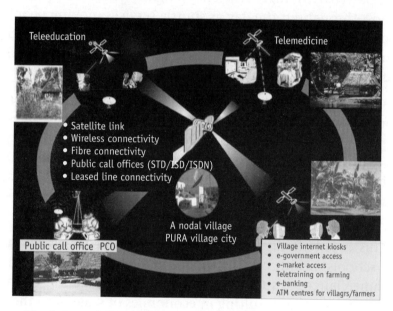

▲ **Fig. 8.6** *PURA—Electronic Connectivity*

Knowledge connectivity (Fig. 8.7) will transform the rural area with connectivity in education, healthcare, vocational training, satellite applications for crops, water and forest management, environment protection and cooperative product marketing. The combination of electronic connectivity and knowledge connectivity will generate literacy movement, teleeducation, healthcare and resource management.

It would be seen therefore that the triad of physical, electronic and knowledge connectivity brings forth the economic connectivity (Fig. 8.8) through small-scale industries, agro and food processing, warehouses, micro

▲ **Fig. 8.7** *PURA—Knowledge Connectivity*

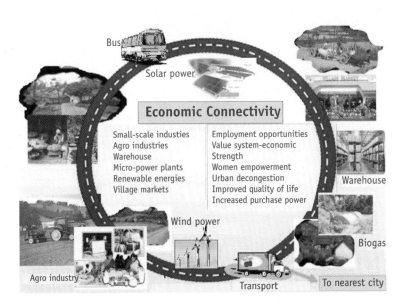

▲ **Fig. 8.8** *PURA—Economic Connectivity*

power plants, renewable energy and village markets. This will generate larger employment opportunities, women empowerment and improved quality of life. The villages not only improve the quality of life but also maintain the rural beauty and environment. Moreover, the connectivities make the rural villages close to any part of the world.

Unified PURA Implementation Strategy

PURA has to be a business proposition which is economically viable and managed by entrepreneurs and small-scale industrialists, as it involves education, health, power generation, transport and management. PURA needs an integrated development approach with empowered management structure. The integrated implementation strategy is brought out in Fig. 8.9.

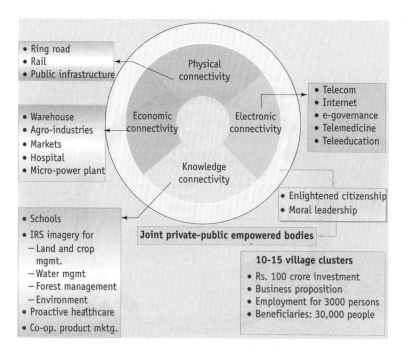

Fig. 8.9 *Unified PURA Implementation Strategy*

STRONG AND SELF-RELIANT INDIA

We have so far considered various sectors of development and the profile of a knowledge society, its multiple components, and the requisite system integration and the missions. We need to integrate these missions with the core strengths of the nation to achieve the desired goals. A nation's strengths predominantly reside in its natural and human resources. In natural resources, India is endowed with a vast coastline with marine resources as well as oil wealth. In minerals, apart from conventional material resources, it is well-known that India has the largest deposits of titanium, beryllium and tungsten. India ranks among the top few nations having a rich biodiversity. Particularly, in the herbal area there are potential applications for developing multiple products for nutrition, prevention and cure of diseases. The global herbal product market of $ 61 billion, India must have a leading share. There is tremendous opportunity for growth in this area. India has similar potential for promoting floriculture and aquaculture in a big way.

Knowledge-based value addition for these natural resources would mean exporting value-added products rather than merely the raw materials. Use of IT for commercialisation and marketing can increase our outreach and speed enormously. Ancient knowledge is a unique resource of India for it has the treasure of over 5000 years of civilisation. It is essential to leverage this wealth for national well-being, as well as, to seek global presence for the nation.

Human resources, particularly the 300 million young population, are the unique core strength of the nation. This resource can be transformed through various educational and training programmes. Skilled, unskilled and creative manpower can be transformed into wealth generators particularly in the service sectors, agro-industries etc. (Fig. 8.10).

Human resources, particularly the 300 million young population, are the unique core strength of the nation. This resource can be transformed through various educational and training programmes.

Knowledge-intensive industries can be generated out of our existing industries by injecting demand for high-level software/hardware, which would bring tremendous value addition. It is said, "the precious asset for a company or a country is the skill, ingenuity and imagination of its people. With globalisation, this will become more important because everybody will have access to world class technology and the key distinguishing feature will be the ability of people in different countries to use their imagination to make the best use of the technology". Indeed development and innovative use of multiple technologies with transparent management structure and coupled with IT, will lead India into a knowledge superpower.

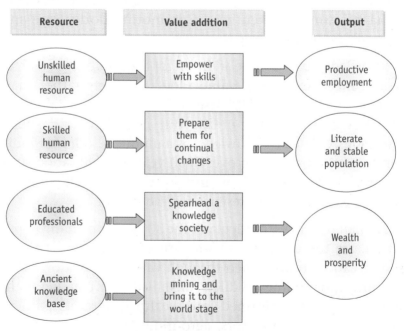

▲   **Fig. 8.10   *Education and Human Empowerment***

With our civilisational heritage and core strengths of large natural and human resources, with value addition and launching mission projects, desired goals of food, health, and social security, economic prosperity and national

Human resources, particularly 300 million young population, are the unique core strength of the nation. This resource can be transformed through various educational and training programmes.

security can be achieved, leading to Developed India by 2020 (Fig. 8.11) and rightful place in the world.

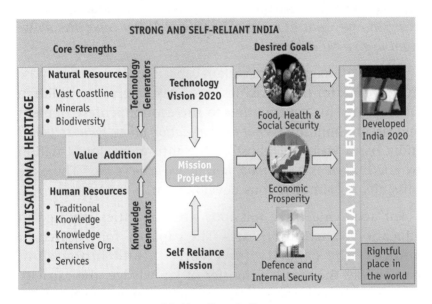

Fig. 8.11 *Strong and Self-Reliant India*

CREATIVITY AND MORAL LEADERSHIP

During the interactions with Vice-Chancellors of various universities, professors and teachers, a question on building moral leadership in education was put to them. A professor at Texas A&M University, Dr. Robert Slater, an expert in education and human resource development, accessed the question from the media, and sent an e-mail. Further, he brought out his view of building capacities to the students for nation building during a meeting with him. The analysis of this is summarised here, which is note worthy. Let it spread among the teaching and student communities.

CAPACITIES FOR NATION BUILDING

The most important mission for the nation is the creation of capacities for nation building. In the education environment—a few questions arise, *What kind of human beings do we want to make of ourselves? What capacities do we want to give our students?*

If we want to give them certain capacities, for what purpose must we ask for the capacities? We want to give our children the capacity for contributing to the economic development and nation building. *What kind of nation do we want to build?* India has a vision of transforming into a developed nation by 2020. *There is a roadmap, how do we achieve this?* There are missions for simultaneous development.

For achieving these missions, the capacities required in educational institutions are—The capacity for research or enquiry, the capacity for creativity and innovation, particularly the creative transfer of knowledge, the capacity to use high technology, the capacity for entrepreneurial leadership and the capacity for moral leadership.

(a) Research and Enquiry

The 20th Century was for the generation of knowledge. The 21st Century will be about the management of all the knowledge and information we have generated and add value to it. We must give our students, the skills with which they will find a way through the sea of knowledge that we have created. Today, we have the ability through technology, to really and truly teach ourselves and to become the life-long learners that any sustained economic and political development requires.

(b) Creativity and Innovation

Creativity comes from beautiful minds. It can be anywhere and from any part of the country. It has got multiple-dimensions like inventions, discoveries and innovations. Creativity has an attitude to accept change and newness, a willingness to play with ideas and possibilities, a flexibility of outlook, the habit of enjoying the good, while looking for ways to improve it. Creativity involves a process to work hard continually, for improving ideas and solutions by making gradual alterations and refinements to the works. The important aspect of creativity is—seeing the same thing as everybody else, but thinking of something different. These characteristics are required to be nurtured and promoted amongst the students.

(c) Capacity to use High Technology

Every student in our university should graduate to using the latest technologies for aiding their learning process. Universities should equip themselves with the tools like computer hardware, software, laboratory equipment, and internet facilities and provide an environment for the students to enhance their learning ability through a digital library.

(d) Entrepreneurial Leadership

Entrepreneurial leadership first involves identifying the problem and then finding its solution in the context of development. Entrepreneurship starts with understanding our needs and realising that, as human beings we all have similar needs. It begins with wanting to help others as we help ourselves. Secondly, there should be a willingness to undertake new challenges. Entrepreneurship requires doing things differently, being bold in our thinking—which is always risky. We must teach our children to take calculated risks for the sake of a larger gain. The third part involves the disposition to do things right.

(e) Moral Leadership

Moral leadership requires the ability to have compelling and powerful dreams or vision for human betterment, and disposition to do the right thing and influence others also to do the right thing.

(f) Perfect Learner

If all the five attributes are inculcated in a student, by his principal, by his teacher, by his parents, he will have a burning desire to learn throughout his life, and also set an example for others. A perfect learner will not only learn from the class room, but the environment as well. I firmly believe that the teacher's mission is to generate **perfect learners**, with the above five attributes.

DEVELOPMENT AND LEADERSHIP CONNECTIVITY

'Developed India', as defined by us, can be powered mainly by economic strength. The economic strength has to be powered by competitiveness and the competitiveness has to be powered by knowledge (Fig. 8.12). Knowledge has to be powered by technology, and technology has to be powered by business. Business has to be powered by innovative management, and management has to be powered by leadership. What are the characteristics of leadership? A leader will neither be a commander nor a super-boss, but a visionary, a facilitator, and a thinker. Above all, the nobility of the mind is the hallmark of the leader. Will this race grow?

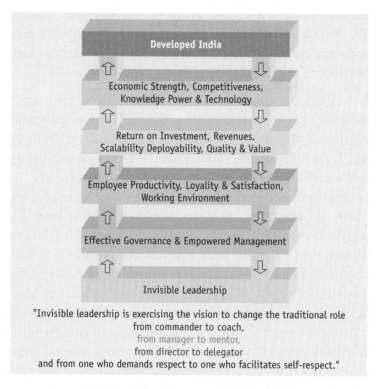

Fig. 8.12 *Development and Leadership–Connectivity*

CONCLUDING REMARKS

India is well-placed at the dawn of the knowledge era. We should not miss this opportunity. Our culture and civilisation have been enriched over the ages by great thinkers who have always taken an integrated view of life as a fusion of mind, body, and intellect. In the coming decades, our youngs will see a confluence of civilisational and modern technological streams.

Young scientists today are in a better position to engage in the pursuit of scientific research, invention and innovation which form the major components of high technology development. It is useful to make a distinction between these elements. Scientific research is concerned with the acquisition of knowledge of the nature of the physical world. Invention is the creation of a new product, process or service or creation of something that is not existent.

The children and youth of India have the unique opportunity to serve the nation through a campaign for a 'Developed India' by 2020, with science and technology as the tool. Indian minds have value systems based on great civilisational strengths and intellectual prowess. With our core competence in certain technologies and thrust for value addition to the natural resources with quality human resource, along with better healthcare and infrastructure, transformation of India into a developed nation is a reality. The technological strengths of a billion people is similar to the radiated energy of the universe. Only dreams lead to thoughts and thoughts result into actions. Action is needed from every citizen to progress the mission of our Developed India vision. Ignited young minds are the powerful engines to achieve the missions. The indomitable spirit of the youth, capacity for nation building and creative leadership will give India, the competitive edge and a rightful place in the world.

Epilogue

We were thinking on how to summarise the book aptly. So far, we have outlined the importance of technology and how its application in select sectors can empower India to become a developed nation. However, development cannot take place in isolation. It has to take place with the active involvement of the people, and the people who will lead the development are today's youth. We decided to get a feedback firsthand from today's educated youth on technology and development. In fact, towards the conclusion of the classes on Technology Management at Anna University, five questions designed by Prof. Kalam, were asked to the students as a part of their examination.

1. *What do we have to do to enable India to enter into G-8 group of nations?*

2. *More than 40 million tonnes of food grains are stocked, which is creating economic stagnation. Why? Analyse the reasons and suggest possible solutions.*

3. *Can you establish the dynamics of leadership with Technology–Industry–Society?*

4. Discuss the distinct features of Agriculture Society, Industrial Society, Information Society and Knowledge Society and explain how feedback mechanism helps in improving these societies.

5. Empowering village clusters is very important for India's Development. Discuss the concept of PURA with reference to PEEK (connectivity).

We thought of reproducing answers from two students for the first two questions.

- **Mr. Rahul Datta Roy, Final Year student of Aero-Engineering Department, MIT had the following to state:**

ANSWER TO QUESTION NO. 1

India as a developed country

I personally think that India has the potential to overtake even the G-8 countries in terms of economic or social development. What we lack is the fire within us to ignite the fuel.

We have the natural resources but we do not utilise them. The various reasons might be poor leadership, lack of value addition, etc.

There is a proverb that an army of lions led by a sheep will lose a battle against an army of sheep led by a lion. The need of the hour is visionary and able leadership which can dispel the darkness of ignorance.

Another impetus to development is provided by literacy. An illiterate nation has never progressed. We should not dream of 'Great India' but 'Literate India'.

I also think that we lack the aggressive instinct to market our goods in the global economy. We are rather taken in by 'Made in

USA'. We should encourage Indian goods and also market them effectively.

We should also identify our biodiversity and see to it, that they are patented.

Also we should keep a check on the growing population menace because increase in quantity will lead to decrease in quality. For this I would suggest the rigorous steps taken by the Chinese Government.

A democratic country, like India can surge ahead of any developed nation once its people take steps together. In physics, if two frequencies match, resonance occurs. Similarly, if the frequency of our thoughts match with one another, as well as concerted actions, then India will emerge as a world power.

ANSWER TO QUESTION NO. 2

Economic Stagnation

As per the statistics, 40 million tonnes of food grains is stocked or rather "wasted". This statistical data is even more alarming when we consider that there are many Indians who barely survive and suffer from hunger and poverty.

I personally think the PDS (Public Distribution System) is to be blamed for this atrocious act.

We have not properly channelled our agricultural products. There are many tribal villages which do not have ration shops. Opening of ration shops there will be a boon.

Also we can export our food grains (although of low nutritional quality) to countries like Somalia or Afghanistan.

The Indian government should also keep the 'Poor Indian' in mind while deciding on the buffer prices.

Next we should try to increase the quality of our agro-products through the latest genetic innovation.

High yielding and nutritious grain varieties can be genetically manufactured.

- **Mr. Kripa Shankar, BE Mining (VIII Semester) had the following to state:**

ANSWER TO QUESTION NO. 1

India as a Developed Country

G-8 countries are the group of developed countries. Though India has got all the potential resource for becoming a developed country, the dream is still not a reality. As I see India has a wealth of traditional knowledge, but it is scattered. We have to compile all those knowledge to make it effective. The developed five sectors should be.

Agricultural sector:

India has a vast fertile land and we stand second in production of cereals and No. 1 in production of fruit but in terms of productivity (yield per hectare) we stand in the 45th position. We need to produce food grains with high nutritional value and quality. We should add value to the agricultural products by using innovative food processing technologies.

Education and Healthcare:

Education is vital for producing brains bestowed with knowledge to give innovative ideas. Unfortunately, the educational system that we have doesn't do this. It should be a sort of Learning and not a Reading or Reproduction process. Education must be rendered to all children in the rural areas. Tele-education can come in handy.

Healthcare sector can be drastically improved by developments in the field of biotechnology. India has a wealth of medicinal herbs, and the biotechnologist must tap these resources, to make it useful to the human race. The vaccine and medicine for AIDS and cancer should be developed in India.

Infrastructure facilities:

Connectivity of all rural areas through roads and electricity must be provided. The programme of PURA (Providing Urban Amenities to Rural Areas) should help in a very big way.

Strategic Sector:

India has advanced quite well in aeronautics and space technology but still after independence it is in the 5th place. We should try to tap solar energy for satellites, and in fact meet our electricity needs from those satellites using Hyperplanes (reusable launch vehicles). Nuclear power should be used for defence purposes.

Information and Communications Technology:

This sector should provide information and connectivity to all the other sectors. The Silicon age is gone. India should look into nanotechnology and make new advancements in this area. Electronics connectivity to all the rural areas should be established and high bandwidth should be provided. Information technology is one of our core competence and we should develop it in a big way.

ANSWER TO QUESTION NO. 2

Economic Stagnation

India produces about 200 million tonnes of food grains every year. By 2020 this amount should be doubled. At present the government's policy is to stock these food grains. The 40 million tonnes stocked led economic stagnation. The reasons are:

- We are trying to be conservative and stocking for future use. But we are not providing it to the poor people who are starving for food.

- *The food grains produced in India are not meeting the international standards, in terms of nutritional value and quality and, hence are not being exported.*

- *We are not doing any value addition to the food grains.*

- *Industries which can do value addition are very few in this country and hence the production is not being consumed.*

Measures to overcome:

- *We should have our own value addition process by developing new industries*

- *Produce food grains which have good nutritional value*

- *We should sell the food grains to the needy people and stock only a sufficient quantity.*

- *Stocking should be done in a good manner, good silos should be used for storing, otherwise they would rot and be of no use.*

Readers would agree and appreciate that developing India has many more Rahul Roys and Kripa Shankers, who are willing to contribute in making India a strong developed nation. It is in the interest of our society and the nation as a whole, that the educated youth—their thoughts and energies—should be properly channelised to make India a developed nation, particularly when we are in an advantageous position with the advent of the knowledge age. This will bring societal transformation with e-education, tele-medicine and e-governance providing an opportunity for a large employment, transparency in administration and rural prosperity.

We must capitalise our strength as a knowledge society to achieve the goals of Developed India by 2020. It is scientists, engineers, technologists, technicians and farmers and others of this country who have to shoulder the responsibility and integrate the efforts into the development missions. Policy makers of our country must help in this process of transforming the missions into actions.

Challenges will always be there, but it is for us to convert them into opportunities for growth and development.

Conclusion

"We need an Indomitable Spirit and Courage to face and learn from failures to succeed in any mission"

THE NATION

Technology, undoubtedly, will play a pivotal role in leading India towards a developed nation. It has been our endeavour in the preceding chapters to show how technology can be used beneficially in the Indian context for transforming India into a developed country. In this process, we have to take the help of certain innovative models and use certain imaginative approaches in the application of technology and in solving problems which plague India.

Nation in its development mode has to go through integrated development plan and empowered management structures in areas such as education, healthcare, agriculture and food processing, biotechnology, information and communication technology, strategic sectors, industries and building-up of infrastructure including power, networking of rivers and rural development through PURA.

The tasks at hand seem to be challenging, but are realisable for a determined nation of one billion people. We should take cognisance of the fact that India, though the largest democracy in the world is still a developing country even after five decades of independence. This situation needs to be changed and India must become a developed country. Let us have the determination and single minded devotion for the cause of development. We should remember that our forefathers had to make a lot of sacrifices, face hardships and difficulties in freeing us from the clutches of foreign rule so that we could live in Independent India and hold our head high. Let us for a moment pause and think that for what we would like to be remembered by our future generations. We will be remembered only if we give to our younger generation a vibrant, prosperous and safe India resulting out of economic prosperity coupled with our civilisation heritage.

> *A nation is great, not because a few people are great, but because everyone in the nation is great.*

A nation is great, not because a few people are great, but because everyone in the nation is great. The young should excel in academics and become good human beings with moral values and societal care. Cohesive and focussed efforts of the youth can see through the challenge to make India a "developed nation". Just like our First Vision of Independence created leaders, we are sure the children and youth will rise to the occasion and become not only the professionals in multiple areas, but also creative entrepreneurs for providing employment opportunity to others. The leaders are the creators of new organisations of excellence. Higher the proportion of creative leaders, higher the potential of success of the vision the **"Developed India"**.

VISION TRANSFORMING TO REALITY

For India to be among the top six developed nations, it has to be economically and commercially powerful. GDP will have to rise above 10%, poverty will have to eradicated and there should be no unemployed people.

Five mega missions discussed in detail, namely agriculture and food processing, education and healthcare, information and communication technology, infrastructure including power and critical technology, and strategic sector must be taken up on a war footing. In addition, river networking, PURA and enriching the village life and tourism are other mission areas needed for development. India has a strong core competence both in terms of natural, and quality human resources in these sectors. The network of inter-relationships in these missions needs to be understood and exploited through a strong partnership between R&D institutions, academia and industries. These partnerships are bound to lead to higher productivity and growth, and in turn lead to the export of state-of-the-art technology products and generate wealth. This vision is indeed a challenge and this can be overcome only if we, the one billion people as a nation come forward and join hands, forgetting all other petty issues.

> *This vision is indeed a challenge and this can be overcome only if we, the one billion people as a nation come forward and join hands, forgetting all other petty issues.*

Government alone cannot face this challenge, it is for us Indians from all walks of life to help in the integration process of transforming the vision into missions, to make India a prosperous, happy, peaceful and secure nation, with a rightful place among comity of nations.

BUILDING LEADERSHIP

Almost, each one of us from our childhood go through the various phases of education. This, over the years brings about the best in each one of us, both in terms of creativity and learning. Empowerment plays the predominant role in shaping us. *How does a child, a teenager, an adult and a leader react to a particular situation?* The child asks, *"What can you do for me?"* The teenager says, *"I want to do it alone"*. The young person proclaims, *"let us do it together"*. The leader offers, *"What can I do for you?"* The child, when empowered by parents, transforms into a responsible citizen. A teacher, empowered with knowledge and experience creates a good human being with strong value systems. When a leader empowers his people, new leaders are born. It is these new leaders, who can greatly influence and bring about the necessary changes in diverse and multiple areas. The transformation of *'what can you do for me'* to *'what can I do for you'* demands vision with an inspiring capability. The best of creativity among the students will emerge by integrated influence of teachers and parents on them. Empowerment at various levels through the power of knowledge is the key to the transformation of developed India.

The most powerful resource on earth is the ignited young mind and we believe that it should be empowered with adequate knowledge and leadership qualities to make the developed India dream—a reality.

MORAL LEADERSHIP

Moral leadership involves two things. First it requires the ability to have a compelling and powerful dream or vision of human betterment. A state in which human beings could be better off in the future than they are now. Secondly, where entrepreneurial leadership requires people to acquire the habit of doing things right, moral leadership requires a disposition to do the right thing and influence others also to do the right thing.

INDOMITABLE SPIRIT

For success in any mission what we need is leaders with an indomitable spirit. That should be the mission of any educational centres. Let us study the characteristics of the indomitable spirit. It has two components. The first component is that there must be a Vision leading to higher goals of achievement. I would like to recall a couplet from *Thirukkural* by the Poet Saint Thiruvalluvar written 2500 years ago.

வெள்ளத் தனைய மலர்நீட்டம் மாந்தர்தம்
உள்ளத் தனைய துயர்வு

(Vellath thanaiya malarneetam maandhartham Ullath thanaiya thuyarvu)

It means that whatever may be the depth of the river or lake or pond, whatever may be the condition of the water, the lily flower always comes out and blossoms. Similarly, the man succeeds if there is a determination to achieve a goal even if it is apparently impossible to achieve.

Many of us have gone through large programmes, projects, technologies and scientific teachings. We would have experienced that success is not in sight and that there are many hurdles. The same poet reminds us at this point of time through another couplet:

இடும்பைக் கிடும்பை படுப்பர் இடும்பைக்
கிடும்பை படாஅ தவர்

(Idumbai kidumbai paduppar idumbai Kidumbai padaa thavar)

It means successful leaders can never be defeated by problems. They become masters of the situation and defeat the problems. These two Thirukkurals characterise the indomitable spirit.

Whether a school or an engineering student, there is an unlimited degree of quest for knowledge among the nation's youth. It is the national spirit among the youth to do something for India that should be taken in the right spirit and a national consensus to be evolved to work in a coherent manner towards achieving the aim of developed India. This necessitates taking full advantage of technology in the identified missions, with transparency in administration and management. This would need political will and real time decision-making process, all for the much larger purpose of making nation proud. We suggest that the political parties, in their manifesto specifically include the action plans and the speed with which the party will realise the developed India.

We would like to re-emphasise that vision India 2020 is achievable. One billion indian people are now looking towards the political leaders for providing the political directions to the nation. It is time, our political parties compete with each other in realising Developed India—a nation with economic prosperity and civilisational heritage before the year 2020. **This will be a beautiful India, prosperous India and safe India. Let us work together towards this endeavour for which we will be remembered by our future generation.**

Design of Satellite Launch Vehicles
Recollection of SLV-3 Experience

INTRODUCTION

Space Technology in India was initiated in 1963 by Dr Vikram Sarabhai with a vision of India's own communication spacecraft launch capability in 1980s. Since then, more than 3000 test rockets, meteorological rockets and sounding rockets have been designed, built and launched.

The meteorological rockets can carry 10 kg to an altitude of 60 km and the sounding rockets can put 100 kg class of payload to an altitude of 300–400 km (Fig. I.1). This base of sounding rocket technology was the first design and technology foundation for SLV-3—India's first satellite launch vehicle. SLV-3 development paved the way for indigenous design, capability, technology development and led to the evolution of ASLV, PSLV, GSLV during the subsequent years of aerospace programme management methods.

SLV-3 Flight test on July18, 1980

*Prof. Satish Dhawan congratulating
Dr. Kalam on the successful test of SLV-3*

LAUNCH VEHICLE DESIGN

Launch Vehicle design and development is highly interactive involving multiple disciplines and technologies. The SLV-3

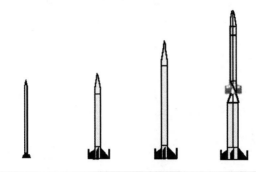

Features	RH-200	RH-300	RH-300 MK II	RH-560 MK II
No. of stages	2	1	1	2
Length (m)	3.6	4.8	4.9	7.7
Lift-off weight (kg)	108	370	510	1350
Payload Wt. (kg)	10	60	70	100
Altitude (km)	85	100	150	550
	Meteorology	Middle	Middle	Ionosphere
	Application	Atmosphere	Atmosphere	

▲ **Fig. I.1 Sounding Rockets of ISRO**

class launch vehicle is designed to inject a satellite in a low earth orbit which needs a minimum velocity of 7.88 km/sec. The satellite has to be injected at an altitude of 300 km and at an inclination of 45° to the equator (Figure I.2). To do this function, the main energy source is the four solid rocket motors. The solid rocket motors with their control system, heat shield, satellite and attitude control system and instrumentation are sequenced and the flight path is controlled, based on attitude reference input processed and fed to the control system for the required control force. SLV-3 employs open loop guidance with stored pitch programme to steer the vehicle in flight along the pre-determined trajectory. The rocket motor propellant grains with a peak vacuum thrust of 54 tonnes. First stage of SLV-3 have been designed for the required ballistic performance and structurally integrated including viscoelastic analysis. The other three stage rocket motors thrust rating are about 29T, 9T and 2T. The heat shield protects the fourth stage rocket motor and the satellite from aerodynamic heating.

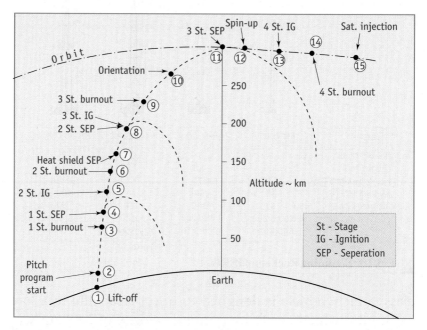

▲ **Fig. I.2   Flight Sequence—Earth to Orbit**

The launch vehicle during its flight passes through various flight regimes like subsonic, transonic, supersonic and hypersonic, finally achieving the required injection velocity. Aerodynamic, thermal and structural design for launch vehicle structures had been carried out for both static and dynamic loads, which the launch vehicle would experience during its ascent phase.

SLV-3 has 44 major sub-systems with 100,000 components both mechanical, electrical, electromechanical and chemical. Figure I.3 presents the exploded view of SLV-3. The total design, apart from individual components and systems, took into account the interface requirements between the stages and systems. From the drawing board to launch, it is

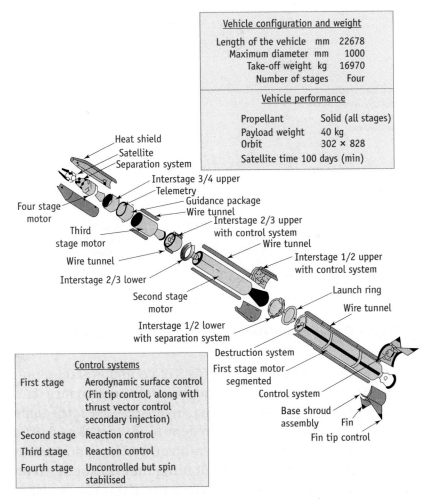

Vehicle configuration and weight

Length of the vehicle	mm	22678
Maximum diameter	mm	1000
Take-off weight	kg	16970
Number of stages		Four

Vehicle performance

Propellant	Solid (all stages)
Payload weight	40 kg
Orbit	302 × 828
Satellite time 100 days (min)	

Heat shield
Satellite
Separation system
Interstage 3/4 upper
Telemetry
Guidance package
Four stage motor
Wire tunnel
Interstage 2/3 upper with control system
Third stage motor
Wire tunnel
Wire tunnel
Interstage 2/3 lower
Interstage 1/2 upper with control system
Second stage motor
Launch ring
Wire tunnel
Interstage 1/2 lower with separation system
Destruction system
First stage motor segmented
Control system
Base shroud assembly
Fin
Fin tip control

Control systems

First stage	Aerodynamic surface control (Fin tip control, along with thrust vector control secondary injection)
Second stage	Reaction control
Third stage	Reaction control
Fourth stage	Uncontrolled but spin stabilised

▲ **Fig. I.3** *Exploded View of SLV-3*

essential for launch vehicle designers to conceive the functions of each component relating to sub-system, system performance and interfacing ground installations like the automatic checkout system. The development of design and operations software for SLV-3 from the design to launch is given in Fig. I.4.

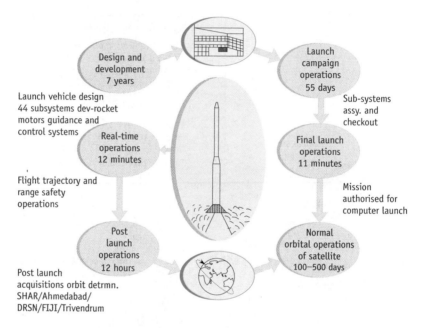

▲ **Fig. I.4** *Development of Design and Operations Software for SLV-3* ■ ■

Automatic checkout system consists of computerised ground telemetry, telecommand, payload, control and guidance and power systems. When the sub-systems are realised at the same time, the automatic checkout system is also developed. The system is then interfaced with on-board systems and various systems functioning is carried out using the checkout system. The launch vehicle is one of the elements of this total mission that has to be integrated with the launch complex, down-range telemetry station and other satellite tracking network and safety systems. From launch vehicle design and development, to the first successful launch, about 50 static tests of rocket motors have been conducted at various environmental conditions and their thrust time performance have been confirmed with prediction. Three types of control systems (Fin Tip Control (FTC), Thrust Vector Control (TVC), Reaction Control System (RCS)) of eight packages with thousands of thrusters/control components have been evaluated with various instrumentation packages including equipment bay. Also, they have been environmentally tested for actual performance and qualified through seven sounding rocket flights.

Design Tools

Figure I.5 describes, given a mission, how the configuration design is carried out, linking the aerodynamic, structural, propulsion, control and guidance designs. Apart from vehicle performance, the launch vehicle design takes into account, the launch azimuth based on instantaneous impact points and fly-over countries criteria, launch window based on the satellite injection time and the surface and in-flight wind conditions. In addition, during the vehicle development phase, to study the performance of flight, 600 parameters had to be telemetered. The post flight analysis methodology using these telemetered data in real-time was evolved.

For design alone, during seven years (1973–80) about 300 engineers have been working and the total computer time used was about 30,000 hours using various computing systems like the IBM 360/44, PDP 11/34, IRIS-55, EAI 682/PACE-100, etc. For launch vehicle design, various tools were used for aerodynamic design, structural design, control and guidance design, as follows.

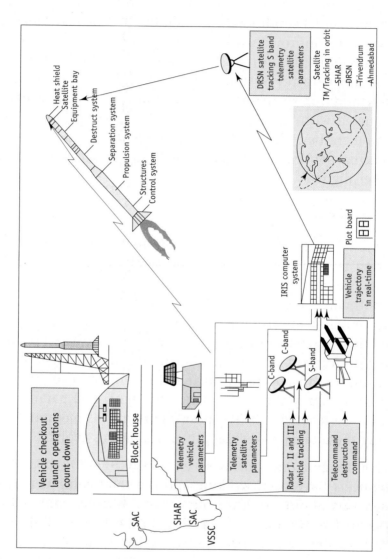

▲ **Fig.I.5   SLV Mission**

AERO-STRUCTURAL DESIGN

About 90 software packages were developed for aerospace design especially in the areas of aerodynamics and structures. Various types of design programs for aerodynamic design were generated including the 6D trajectory simulation program, optimum pitch program, stage separation dynamics, heat shield design packages, post flight analysis, etc. In case of structural analysis, design packages developed include heat shield design, viscoelastic analysis on rocket motors, composite structural design for 3rd and 4th stages, static and vibration flutter analysis of fins. The type of test data that go into launch vehicle design are—the pressure and force measurement from wind tunnel tests at various Mach numbers and in case of structures, kinetic heating simulation of heat shield and structural qualification of various interstages and hydrostatic test of motor cases and gas bottles. Wind tunnel data were used in the various phases of SLV-3 design, especially in the estimation of local loads for structural design, estimation of forces and moments for trajectory simulation studies, thermal protection studies, aeroelastic behaviour due to SLV-3's large L/D (length to diameter) and for the stage separation studies.

CONTROL SYSTEM DESIGN AND SIMULATION

The control system design methodology utilised the short period analysis of linear and non-linear systems to obtain initial disturbance condition response and design the gains for the control system. This was checked with full fledged 6D simulation program with control. Also, the control system design program took into account the flexibility of the vehicle, typical control force requirement, sensor locations, etc. The important study of the simulation was the analysis of failure modes and their impact on range safety aspects. For example, failure of a control electronics during the flight

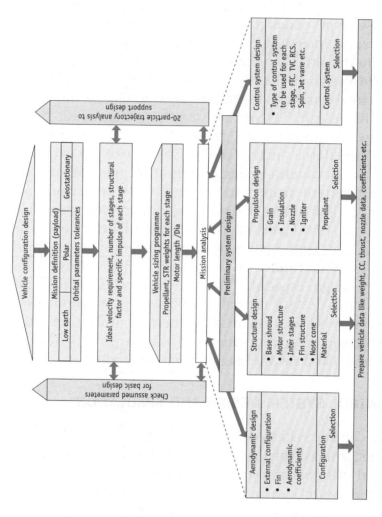

▲ **Fig.I.6 Launch Vehicle—Configuration Design**

sequence, say rate gyro or vehicle attitude program was simulated by hybrid computer system and the results are presented in Fig. I.6. With the flight hardware, detailed hardware-in-the-loop simulation was carried out for the mission. Set-up of hardware-in-the-loop simulation consists of a small digital computer (analog computer) with proper software interfacing with equipment bay and control system. The control system performance and the various sign checks get confirmed for the given mission in the test bed.

DESIGN EXPERIENCES

During the design and development phase of SLV-3 many problems were encountered both in hardware and software. As examples, two of our design experiences are discussed below.

Weld Mismatch Study

The first and second stage rocket motors of SLV-3 are made of high strength steel (100 kg/mm²) and of welded constructions of 3 to 3.5 mm thick sheets and machined forgings. The motor case is fabricated out of shell segments and domes welded with reference to shell to shell or shell to domes. The mismatch is specified as the shift between control axis of the two mating parts. During the design phase, for example, we specified the circumferential mismatch of the welded joints as 0.3 mm. During the fabrication process it was found that with given welding fixture and fabrication methods used, mismatch limit exceeded 0.3 mm. This led to the evolving stress pattern curves for various mismatch condition. About 8 hydrostatic tests were carried out for first stage to measure strains at various mismatch locations. Normally, calculated mismatch stress for a given pressure of 50 kg/cm.sq. will be 3200 micro-strain. The strain with reference to mismatch pattern for motors varies from 3200 to 4200 micro-strain, depending upon the mismatch varying from no mismatch to 0.3 mm. Mismatch was minimised and controlled by proper fabrication methods, tool modifications and introducing mismatch measurement techniques. This mismatch design, is an important input for rocket motor design for any launch vehicle with high D/t (Diameter and thickness) ratio.

SLV-3-E-01 FLIGHT EXPERIENCE

The next major design experience came from the flight test itself. SLV-3-E-01 after a normal first stage flight and stage separation at 72 secs of flight, the vehicle started tumbling resulting in the loss of altitude and velocity (Fig. I.7). Identifying the reason for the deviation led to intensive post flight analysis for a period of six months, deploying 900 manhours and in analysing 3000 flight data records and conducting an additional 75 tests in the component level and one full scale control system test. The failure analysis mechanism and the post flight data analysis were the two important elements in identifying the typical failure modes and also rectifying the same. The failure analysis was carried out in a sequence:

(i) analysis of vehicle tracking data

(ii) post flight telemetry data analysis

(iii) analysis of last eleven minutes of check out data (before launch)

(iv) comparison of above with preflight simulation studies, and

(v) trajectory reconstruction using telemetry data and comparison with track data.

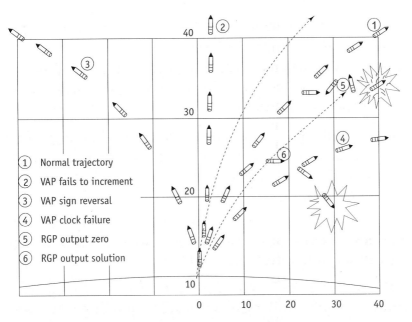

1. Normal trajectory
2. VAP fails to increment
3. VAP sign reversal
4. VAP clock failure
5. RGP output zero
6. RGP output solution

▲ **Fig. I.7** *Typical Failure Mode Consequences*

These analyses by various expert committees finally led to the conclusion that the tumbling flight was due to a hardware malfunction—the solenoid valve of second stage control system failing to close to the command. The failure of the valve was due to dust contamination. Even though, out of 44 sub-systems, 36 sub-systems performed to the mission requirement, one single component failure led to the non-achievement of the mission, that is to inject the satellite in the required orbit. The technical input obtained on thousands of parameters and various specialist teams recommendations resulted in rectifying the defect in the specific component and thus leading to a successful flight, in the next attempt (SLV-3-E-02). The major lessons learnt from the above and corrective actions taken can be summarised as follows:

(a) Failure reporting without any distortion or fear was the main feature of this exercise.

(b) Complete documentation during assembly and other operations should be ensured.

(c) Cleanliness standards should be of high quality and this should be monitored during the various stages of assembly operations.

(d) Failure analysis mechanism adopted should get into the details and exactly pin-point the reasons for failure and the corrective actions to be taken to avoid these problems.

After the successful launch of SLV-3-E2 on July 18, 1980, two more successful missions (SLV3-D-1 & SLV3-D-2) were carried out in May 1981 and April 1983.

SLV-3 programme resulted in significant developments in launch vehicle and mission design, new materials and hardware fabrication technology, solid propellants with high specific impulse, four types of rocket motors, composite heat shield, staging systems, control power plants, inertial sensors, electronics system integration and checkout of launch vehicle, multiple design, simulation and operations software packages and above all system engineering and mission management of satellite launch vehicle. The success of SLV-3 gave confidence to evolve integrated design approach for more complex launch vehicles, such as ASLV, PSLV and GSLV.

Launch Vehicle Integrated Design (LAVID)

Launch Vehicle Design packages have been developed for vehicle sizing, software trajectory optimisation, performance simulation, heat transfer, structural load design analysis, aeroelasticity, structures and control interaction, error-analysis and orbital mechanics. These packages can be integrated with propulsion and control system designs to arrive at an integral design package, termed as 'LAVID'

(Launch Vehicle Integrated Design) (Fig. I.8). It had been assessed that the design of an orbital wing of space shuttle, will take one hour with LAVID, in place of one half-man-year in the conventional design. The major breakthroughs expected from this LAVID in the launch vehicle design were:

(i) multiple launch vehicle designs can be evolved with merits and demerits in shortest span for an overall analysis and evaluation;

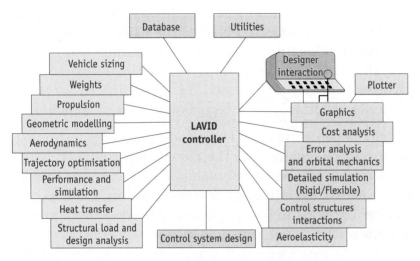

▲ **Fig. I.8** *LAVID—A Launch Vehicle Integrated Design System*

(ii) choice of new technology can be made well in advance;

(iii) design packages will improve the design elements taking into account the integrated design needs.

Based on SLV-3 design and development experiences, LAVID came in handy for future launch vehicle designs.

India subsequently embarked on the development of three major launch vehicle projects based on the technology developed in SLV-3.

1. Augmented Satellite Launch Vehicle (ASLV) capable of placing 150 kg class of satellite in near earth orbit.

2. Polar Satellite Launch Vehicle (PSLV) to orbit 1000 kg class satellite in sun-synchronous polar orbit.

3. Geo-synchronous Satellite Launch Vehicle (GSLV) to inject 2000 kg class of communication and MET setellites in Geo-Transfer Orbit (GTO).

The four launch vehicles are depicted in Fig. I.9. System studies had been carried out on Due-East missions, overcoming the range safety problems to enhance the payload capability of GSLV and achieving INSAT class of missions using PSLV modules with a cryogenic upper stage. The development of cryogenic system became vital for the enhanced capability of launch vehicles and for reduction in cost of launchings.

The cryogenic engine is a vital and cutting edge technology for the space programme. The closed-loop guidance system development is another area of importance. It is used to guide the rocket system in pre-determined trajectory and inject the satellite in the required attitude and altitude with minimum deviation. The closed loop guidance system consists of gyro sensors like rate integrated gyro, servo accelerometer, on-board computer and the most vital link—the guidance software. The country established the capability for manufacturing inertial sensors especially Dry Tuned Gyros and Ring Laser Gyros. This will make guidance scheme in the redundant strap down inertial navigation system meeting higher accuracy of say ± 10 km in orbit altitude and ± 0.2° in inclination. Booster motor recovery is another technology area for reducing the cost of the launch. The technology to specialise will be re-entry dynamics, building recovery tools and onboard recovery mechanisms.

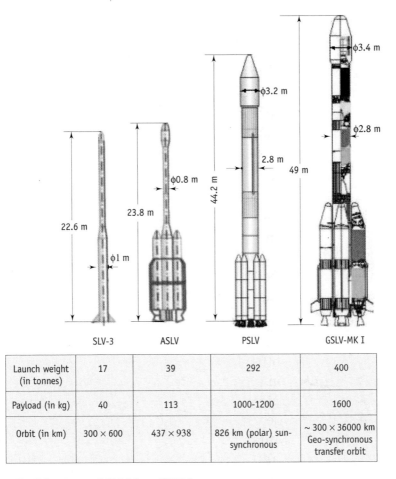

	SLV-3	ASLV	PSLV	GSLV-MK I
Launch weight (in tonnes)	17	39	292	400
Payload (in kg)	40	113	1000-1200	1600
Orbit (in km)	300 × 600	437 × 938	826 km (polar) sun-synchronous	~ 300 × 36000 km Geo-synchronous transfer orbit

▲ **Fig. I.9** *Launch Vehicles of ISRO*

CONCLUDING REMARKS

PSLV, GSLV class of launch vehicles can be used for orbiting larger payloads in low earth orbit. With PSLV, a study has been made, for putting 600 kg of orbiter at 300 km low earth orbit and after the mission is completed, the orbiter can be flown back to earth. This technology will assist in building large space platforms especially for material processing and above all building a capability for future collaboration with nations for solar power satellite.

Integrated Design Approach for Advanced Aerospace Vehicles
A Guided Missile Experience

INTRODUCTION

Advanced Aerospace Vehicle Design requires special design features that should meet the mission requirements of high payload-weight ratio in the case of space launchers and low radar cross-section for specific missiles/aircrafts. The conventional design packages used are discussed in relation to their constraints. Typical examples of interface design are also given. An interactive integrated design approach to eliminate the constraints imposed by individual design modules through interface design modules is discussed. Also, a computer network necessary for an interactive integrated design approach interfacing the mainframe system with CADD System and parallel processing is presented.

Surface to Air Missile in flight

AEROSPACE VEHICLE SYSTEM DESIGN

Recently, a review revealed that the design efforts needed for a launch vehicle system was about 300 man-years and for the missile system about 200 man-years. If the design has to be completed in two years time, atleast 100 designers of various disciplines will be needed and for design of other similar aerospace systems, a number of designers have to be deployed. For a launch vehicle system or missile or aircraft, technical specifications are generated by a team of specialists to meet the mission requirements (Fig. II.1). This leads to sub-system characteristics with different alternatives. After a detailed review and on the basis of experience, the sub-system options are evaluated in the kinematic system model for optimal performance.

Also estimation of reliability and cost would be carried out. This will enable the total system specifications including the sub-system configurations. Subsequently, detailed design of sub-systems are carried out for aerodynamic configuration, airframe, guidance, control and propulsion. The design packages for these sub-systems and the previously generated data banks are utilised in arriving at detailed designs.

Once the sub-system hardware is realised and tested, critical design reviews are carried out with the available test data. Guidance and control hardware and software like inertial navigation system, on-board processor, autopilot go through hardware in loop simulation (HILS) for the detailed performance evaluation. Various sub-systems are integrated and checked out through the flight test. The flight test data is provided to the designers after post flight analysis for further improving the designs. This completes the design cycle which utilise 200 to 300 man-years based on the missile and launch vehicle experience.

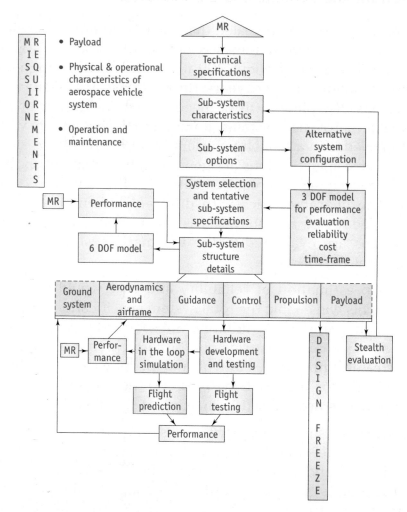

▲ **Fig. II.1** *System Design*

The focus is on linking the various sub-system level design packages and their integration into a total system design package for the aerospace vehicle. Our experience shows that the number of design man-years have been high since the design of the sub-systems is done through sequential rather than parallel operations. A six degree of freedom trajectory run for the evaluation of a typical system with sub-system modules numbering about 200 takes about an hour on a third generation computer system.

To arrive at the final design by incorporating the failure module analysis to arrive at the final design by incorporating the failure module analysis. Also each design package, e.g. aerodynamic design, starts with certain constraints followed by the subsequent design like structural design. Hence these constraints are not seen together in a sequential design process. It is essential that the system constraints are seen in totality so that unrealistic constraints can be removed during the integrated design process.

INTERFACE DESIGN MODULES

On the basis of the design efforts, three typical design packages and modules are considered for interfacing conventional design modules:

(i) Aero-propulsion interaction for a Ramjet

(ii) Structure-control interaction of a typical missile

(iii) Integrated electrical-structural design

These modules focus on the sub-system level interactions and to be taken care of in the integrated design approach.

Aero-Propulsion Interaction for a Ramjet

The integrated design of aero-propulsion system like the Ramjet needs multi-design packages such as vehicle body flow-field analysis, air-intake internal flow-field analysis, analysis of the interaction of multiple intakes, combustor flow-field analysis and matching of combustor and intake operations.

For high performance axi-symmetric intake of Ram rocket system operating up to Mach 3 and angle of attack up to 5 deg., the typical critical pressure recovery for the intake alone will be of the order of 0.82 at starting [Fig. II.2(a)]. However, as can be seen from Fig. II.2(b), when the fuselage is integrated with the air intakes, the critical pressure recovery for the same Mach No. and angle of attack reduces to 0.65 for a cruciform configuration of 4 air-intakes positioned at 45 deg. from vertical. Figure II.2(c) gives the variation of fuel flow-rate with time for matching of the intake to the combustor. In such a system, where the propulsion performance is matched with aerodynamic pressure recovery, the specific impulse obtained from Fig. II.2(d) for Integrated Ram Rocket System with a pressure recovery of 0.6 is about 580 sec. The specific impulse is therefore twice that of the conventional rocket propulsion system. The above example suggests how the propulsion, aerodynamic and combustion phenomena are all interlinked and the need for the designer to have an insight to the mechanism of the three sub-systems.

Structure-Control Interaction of Typical Missile

Many of the guided and controlled missiles have to be designed for flexibility of the airframe due to flight loads, engine deflections, etc. As a missile, has a flexible configuration, to start with the control system designers use normally rigid vehicle approximation and then by iterative process. The effect of flexible vehicle configuration on control system design is considered after flexible data of airframe becomes available. Bending mode shape for a typical missile is given in Fig. II.3(a). For control system designer, the first input is the type of structural frequency variation with respect to time of flight as shown in Fig. II.3(b). The possible design is normally based on moderate class of joints at intersections. The structural frequency will be of the order of 30 Hz and

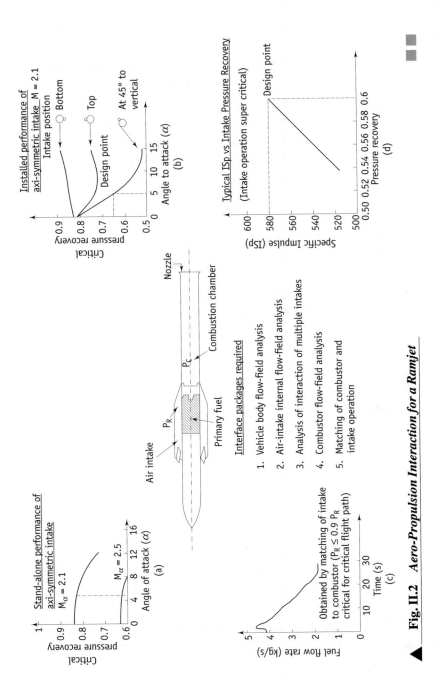

Fig. II.2 *Aero-Propulsion Interaction for a Ramjet*

this needs to be separated from the control frequency by a factor of atleast 4 in order to make the compensator design possible. In Fig. II.3(c), the control system performance of a rigid vehicle, an uncompensated flexible vehicle and compensated flexible vehicle is shown. It is seen that if the vehicle is flexible, the control system gain margin is reduced. If the flexibility effects are not addressed during the design of control system, the response of the in-flight control system becomes oscillatory leading to instability at certain flight conditions along the trajectory. Hence, it is essential to integrate the control system design package and the structural design so that the compensated control system is possible with sufficient gain margins.

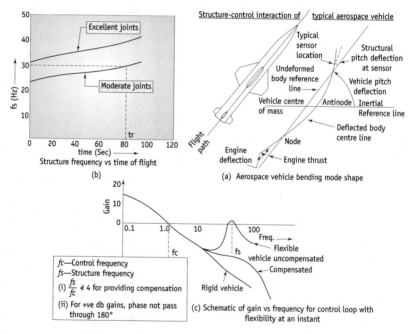

Fig. II.3   ***Structure-Control Interaction of a Typical Aerospace Vehicle***

Integrated Electrical-Structural Design

The antenna system of the homing seeker for a typical missile system is housed in a composite radome. While the radome has to meet the aerodynamic shape and structural requirements, the design of the radome structure is also driven by acceptable near-field antenna pattern with minimum loss. In order to meet the above requirement, the thickness of the structure is obtained by taking into consideration the dielectric constant and loss tangent of the radome material. The shell thickness established from electrical considerations, as shown in Fig. II.4, is then analysed for buckling and bending behaviour. The typical shape of radome is a tangent ogive with L/D ratio of 2.5 to 3 as shown in Fig. II.5(a). The designer has many choices for radome material from glass-polyester, glass-epoxy, glass-polyamide to ceramic for various Mach Nos. and temperature range of 100 to 600 deg. C as shown in Fig. II.5(b). The designer can select the glass-epoxy radome or ceramic radome depending upon the loss tangent requirement for electrical design. As can be seen in Figs. II.5(c) and (d), for glass epoxy, the loss tangent rapidly increases with temperature and also the dielectric constant is high, whereas for ceramic, the rate of increase is much lower. Based on the mission requirement, weight and temperature constraints, a selection has to be made on ceramic radome or glass epoxy radome as discussed in Fig. II.6(a). It can be seen from the radiation pattern of the antenna without radome, the received power is about – 20 dB and with glass-epoxy radome it is about – 28 dB. The most important performance requirement is also to minimise the side lobe of radiation pattern. For a fused silica ceramic radome, the side lobe is lower compared to the glass-epoxy radome. The designers have to translate these factors into electro-mechanical design. This experience needs to be validated and built in to the design package.

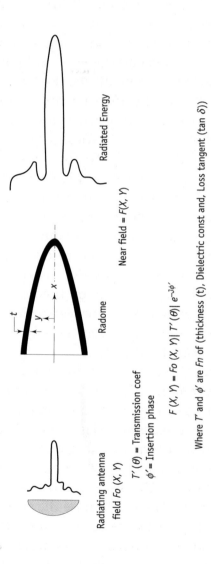

Radiating antenna
field *Fo* (X, Y)

Radome

Near field = *F*(X, Y)

Radiated Energy

$T'(\theta)$ = Transmission coef

ϕ' = Insertion phase

$$F(X, Y) = Fo\,(X, Y)\,|\,T'(\theta)\,|\,e^{-j\phi'}$$

Where T' and ϕ' are *Fn* of (thickness (t), Dielectric const and, Loss tangent (tan δ))

- Obtain *t* as *Fn* of X to get acceptable near-field pattern

- Check for strength   Buckling   Bending

- Finalise *t*

▲   **Fig. II.4**   *Integrated Electrical-Structural Design*

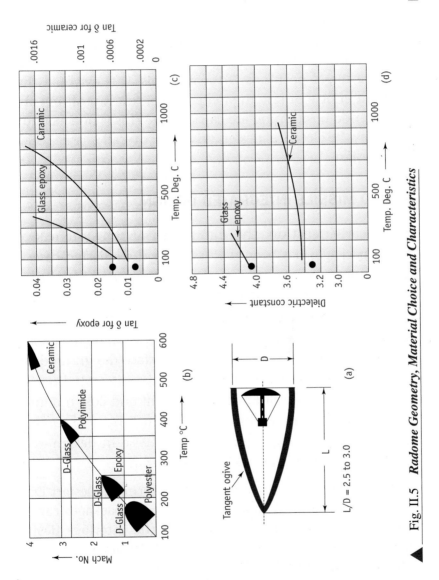

Fig. II.5   Radome Geometry, Material Choice and Characteristics

In the case of guidance, the choice of guidance law has to be chosen suitably to reduce the miss-distance to a minimum. For a typical Surface-to-Air-Missile, a 5 metre miss-distance will result from radome slope of 0.07 as shown in Fig. II.6(b). For a given radome slope as defined in Figs II.6(c) and (d), it is essential to get minimum aberration angle, i.e., the angle between line of sight to the actual and the line of sight to apparent target positions. To realise this, it is essential that the right choice of radome material, thickness profiling and the antenna positioning are carried out. This is one example as to how the electrical design drives the overall missile seeker head design.

GUIDED MISSILE INTEGRATED DESIGN

In the earlier section, the interaction of sub-system level design packages has been discussed for three design cases—aero-propulsion, control-structure and electrical-structural design. In an integrated design approach for an advanced aerospace vehicle, 6 individual design modules with the system constraints as inputs along with the required database have to be built and as many as 6 interface design modules are to be integrated with the interactive integrated design (core) package, in addition to the weight and cost modules. The most important additional links which have to come in are the designers' experience and expertise in design—can these be converted into realistic algorithm?

These need to be converted in the form of Design Data Base so that the individual design software packages can be made to talk to each other through the interface design modules and the interactive integrated design module. The interactive integrated design module shown in Fig. II.7 will remove the constraints normally introduced by individual design modules like aerodynamics, structures, control and

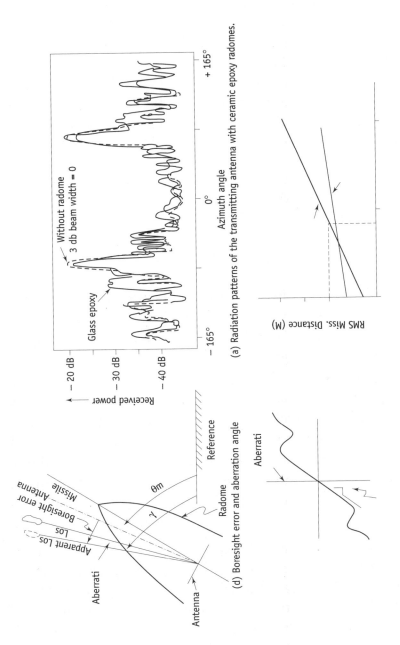

(a) Radiation patterns of the transmitting antenna with ceramic epoxy radomes.

(d) Boresight error and aberration angle

Fig. II.6   Radome Guidance-Performance

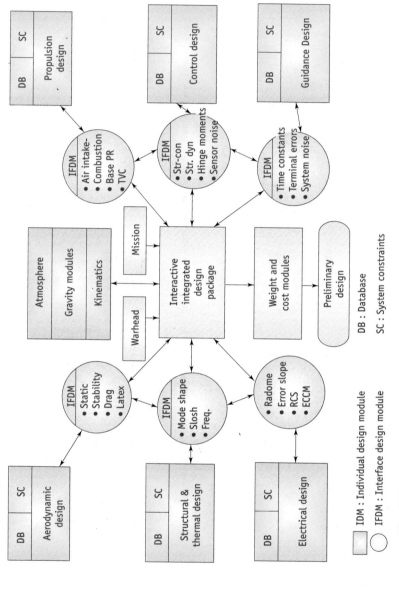

Fig. II.7 *Aerospace Vehicle Integrated Design*

IDM : Individual design module
IFDM : Interface design module

DB : Database
SC : System constraints

guidance systems through interface with major interface design modules. Interactive integrated design approach will bring a reduction of design cycle time to one fifth and, at the same time, the design will be built on experience.

The interactive integrated design approach requires an extensive computational effort and sophisticated computing facilities covering mainframe system, CADD system, parallel processors, etc. The computer network for an integrated design approach is presented in Fig. II.8. In this network, the mainframe system will have interactive terminals through a network processor. The kinematics and the interactive design interface modules are housed in this system. The network processor is interfaced with a CADD system with an ethernet for as many as 18 CADD servers. Each CADD server is provided with 4 disk packs each of 500 MB storage space and also with 8 User Work Stations. The sub-system designs are generated in the CADD centre which has an interactive graphic display. Parallel processors are also interfaced with the network processor of the mainframe system through a front-end processor and they are utilised for major number crunching operations that are normally required for aerodynamic, combustion and structural analysis. Parallel processing of major individual design modules will help to bring down the computational delay on the mainframe system and also on the CADD system. A communication is also established between the parallel processor and the CADD system through the mainframe system. Such a computer network facility is an essential requirement for an integrated design approach. With the emergence of PACE ++ 128 node parallel processing computing system and advanced software codes for Computational Fluid Dynamics (CFD), the integrated and interactive design for guided missile provides tremendous advantage.

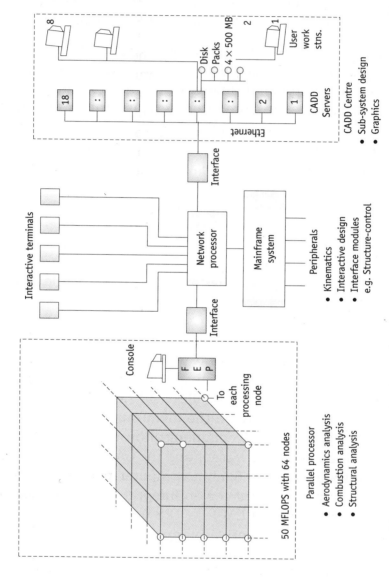

▲   **Fig. II.8   *Computer Network for Integrated Design***

CONCLUDING REMARKS

A conventional design approach for the sub-system of a guided missile resulted in long design cycle time because of sequential and iterative design steps. Also the existing methods introduced constraints into the designs. The three design modules explained in this case study establish the need for an integrated and interactive system design approach, where interfacing of more than one sub-system is involved for complex guided missiles and aerospace vehicles. The availability of large parallel computing systems and Computational Fluid Dynamics (CFD) software will further augment integrated design approach.

References

1. Abdul Kalam, APJ, and YS Rajan, *India 2020—A Vision for the New Millennium*, Penguin India, 1998.

2. Y S Rajan, *Empowering Indians: With Economic, Business and Technology Strengths for the 21st Century*, Har Anand Publications, 2001.

3. Abdul Kalam, APJ, and Arun Tiwari, *Wings of Fire: An Autobiography of APJ Abdul Kalam*, South Asia Books, 1999.

4. Abdul Kalam, APJ, *Ignited Minds: Unleashing the Power within India*, Viking Penguin India, 2002.

5. Abdul Kalam, APJ, *Launch Vehicle Technology: A Perspective*, Technical note no. ISRO-TN-21-81.

6. Abdul Kalam, APJ, *'Design of Satellite Launch Vehicles'*, J. Aeronautical Soc. India, Vol. 34, No. 3–4, 1982.

7. Abdul Kalam, APJ, *Large Boosters for Space Missions*, Technical note No. ISRO-HQ-TN-26-82.

8. Abdul Kalam, APJ, and A Sivathanu Pillai, *Performance & Cost Effectiveness of ISRO Launchers*, Technical note no. ILV/S-TN-01-83.

9. Pillai, A Sivathanu, and S Dhawan, *'Future ISRO Launchers'*, Report No. ISRO/ILV/S:TN:32:85/S.

10. Abdul Kalam, APJ, Prahlada, and B S Sarma, *Integrated Design Approach for Advanced Aerospace Vehicles*, Sadhana, Vol. 12, Part 3, March 1998.

11. Abdul Kalam, APJ, *Lecture on 'Advanced Composites for Aerospace'*, International Conference on Advances in Composite Materials (ICACM-90), 1990.

12. Narasimha R, and APJ, Abdul Kalam, *Development in Fluid Mechanics and Space Technology,* Indian Academy of Sciences, 1988.

13. Abdul Kalam, APJ, *Lecture on 'Mobilising and Challenging Young Scientist for Extraordinary Accomplishments: Story of SLV-3, Prithvi and Agni',* Indian Science Congress Association,1990.

14. Pillai, A Sivathanu, *'102 Degree Launch Azimuth for Geo-Synchronous Missions from SHAR'*—Feasibility Study Report, ISRO, 1983.

15. Pillai, A Sivathanu, *'Optimal Geo-Synchronous Launcher for ISRO'—A Study,* ISRO, 1983.

16. 'Some Experiments in Launch Vehicle Design and Outlook for Future—A Report', VSSC, 1981.

17. Pitroda, Sam, *Vision, Values & Velocity, Silicon India,* 2001.

18. Abdul Kalam, APJ, *India as Knowledge Superpower: A Master Plan.*

19. *'India as Knowledge Superpower—Strategy for Transformation, Recommendations of the Task Force',* Planning Commission, Government of India.

20. *'Report of the Steering Committee on Science & Technology for the Tenth Five Year Plan (2002–2007)',* Planning Commission, Government of India, No.14, 2001.

21. *'Contribution from Different Sectors to GDP and Work Force: Year 2012',* A note from Planning Commission.

22. Parthasarathi, Ashok, *Managing the Knowledge Economy—Opportunities and Challenges of the Emerging Knowledge Economy.*

23. Abdul Kalam, APJ, *Transformation of India into a Knowledge Society,* IISc, Bangalore, August 2001.

24. Abdul Kalam, APJ, *Lecture on 'Transforming India into a Developed Nation—Role of Entrepreneurs',* Global CEO Summit, Kochi, September 2003.

25. Pillai, A Sivathanu, *Lecture on 'The Vision: "Developed India"—An Overview',* Global CEO Summit, Kochi, September 2003.

26. Abdul Kalam, APJ, *'India My Dream: Dynamics of Development',* Lecture by HMA, June 2003.

27. Pillai, A Sivathanu, *Strong and Self Reliant India — Strategy Sector,* Lecture Series *"India My Dream"* Hyderabad Management Association, December 2002.

28. Bajaj, H L, *Strategies for Indian Power Sector Development,* Lecture Series *"India My Dream"* Hyderabad Management Association, December 2002.

29. Rao, P Rama, *The Role of Higher Education in Nation Building,* Lecture Series *"India My Dream"* Hyderabad Management Association, December 2002.

30. Pillai, A Sivathanu, *Advances in Missile Technology, Dr. Biren Roy Trust Lecture,* Aeronautical Society of India, January 2000.

31. Pillai, A Sivathanu, *Advances in Aerospace Technology, Dr. Vikram Sarabhai Memorial Lecture,* Birla Institute of Technology, Ranchi, February 2001.

32. Pillai, A Sivathanu, *Aerospace Systems Development and Manufacturing—Vision, Technology & Strategy,* Aeronautical Society of India, March 2002.

33. Gopalaswamy, R, Pillai, A Sivathanu, Gollakota, S, Venugopalan P, and M Nagarathinam, *Concept Definition and Design of a Single Stage To Orbit Launch Vehicle—Hyperplane,* .

34. Gopalaswamy, R, *Solar Electric Power Generation from Outer Space and its Transmission to Earth.*

35. Nansen, R, *Solar Power Satellites—Energy for the 21st Century—Economic Implications.*

36. Nansen, R, *Sun Power: Global Solution for Coming Energy Crisis,* Ocean Press, 1995.

37. *The International Space Station Commercialization (ISSC) Study,* Potomac Institute for Policy Studies, March 1997.

38. *Indian Space Programme,* Space Forum, Vol. 5, Nos. 1–3, 2000.

39. *Advanced Sensors,* Technology Vision 2020, TIFAC.

40. *Agro-Food Processing—Milk, Cereals, Fruits & Vegetables,* Technology Vision 2020, TIFAC.

41. *Chemical Process Industries,* Technology Vision 2020, TIFAC.

42. *Civil Aviation,* Technology Vision 2020, TIFAC.

43. *Electric Power,* Technology Vision 2020, TIFAC.

44. *Electronics & Communication,* Technology Vision 2020, TIFAC.

45. *Engineering Industries,* Technology Vision 2020, TIFAC.

46. *Food & Agriculture,* Technology Vision 2020, TIFAC.

47. *Health Care,* Technology Vision 2020, TIFAC.

48. *Life Sciences & Biotechnology,* Technology Vision 2020, TIFAC.

49. *Materials & Processing,* Technology Vision 2020, TIFAC.

50. *Road Transportation,* Technology Vision 2020, TIFAC.

51. *Services,* Technology Vision 2020, TIFAC.

52. *Strategic Industries,* Technology Vision 2020, TIFAC.

53. *Telecommunications,* Technology Vision 2020, TIFAC.

54. *Waterways,* Technology Vision 2020, TIFAC.

55. *Driving Forces—Impedances,* Technology Vision 2020, TIFAC.

56. Indiresan, P V, *Report on 'Urbanisation',* 2000.

57. Narasimha, R, *Rockets in Mysore and Britain,* NAL & IISc, 1750–1850 AD Project Document No. DU 8503.

58. Rao, G V, *Spin-offs of Defence Technology,* Mayank Dwivedi et al., National Symposium on Developments in Advanced Composites and Structures, 1994.

59. *IT Task Force,* Basic Background Report, http://www.allindia.com/gov/it-taskforce/.

60. *Indian Software Scenario, e-Commerce— The New Mantra in India and the McKinsey Study for NAS,* http://216.147.108.44/.

61. Kameshwar, C Wali, *Chandra: A Biography of S Chandrasekar,* University of Chicago Press, 1992.

62. Kurien, Varghese, *An Unfinished Dream,* Tata McGraw-Hill, 1997.

63. Raj, Gopal, *Reach for the Stars,* Viking, 2000.

64. *In Search of India's Renaissance,* Centre for Research in Rural and Industrial Development, Chandigarh, Vol. I, 1998.

65. Clark, Norman, Perez-Trejo, Francisco, and Peter M Allen, Edward Elgar Publ, *Evolutionary Dynamics and Sustainable Development—A Systems Approach,* 1995.

66. Chase, Richard B, Nicholas, J, Acquilano and F. Robert Jacob, *Production and Operations Management, Manufacturing & Services,* McGraw-Hill 1998.

67. Little, Richard, L, *Welding and Welding Technology,* Tata McGraw-Hill, 1973.

68. Chowdhury, Subir, *Management in 21 Century,* Financial Times, Prentice-Hall, 2000.

69. Hesselbein, Frances, Goldsmith, Marshall, and Beckhard Richard, *The Leader of the Future,* Jossey-Bass Publishers, 1996

70. Venkatasubramanian, K, *Transformation of India— India as a Knowledge Superpower—Strategies for Actions,* Vikas, 2002.

71. Drucker, Peter, F, *Managing the Next Society,* Truman Talley Books, 2002.

72. *Aerospace Composites: Challenges and Opportunities,* Interline Publishing, 1993.

73. Bronowski, J, *The Ascent of, Man,* Little Brown & Co., 1976.

74. Gulati, Mukesh, *Agenda for Change Developing the Small Scale Industry in India—Need for a Broader Vision,* Allied Publishers, 2000.

75. *Handbook of Systems Engineering and Management,* John Wiley & Sons, 1999.

76. *Aircraft Flight Control and Simulation,* NAL-UNI Lecture Series No. 10, August 1997.

77. Nanus, Burt, *Visionary Leadership,* Jossey-Bass Publishers, 1992.

78. Joshy, Padmanabh K, *Vikram Sarabhai the Man and His Vision,* Mapin Publishers, 1992.

79. David, Bajer, *The Rocket, The History and Development of Rocket and Missile Technology,* New Cavendish Books, 1978.

80. Keegan, John, *A History of Warfare,* Vintage Books, 1993.

81. Lee, R G et. al., *Guided Weapons,* Brassey's Defence Publishers, 1988.

82. Jonathan, Schell, *The Gift of Time,* Penguin, 1998.

83. Spear, Percival, *A History of India,* Penguin Reprint, Vol. II, 1990.

84. Thapar, Romila, *A History of India,* Penguin Reprint, Vol, I 1990.

85. Venkataraman, G, *Bhabha and His Magnificent Obsessions,* Universities Press, 1994.

86. Winter, Frank H, *The First Golden Age of Rocketary,* Smithosonian, 1990.

87. Paroda, R S, Varma, Anupam, and Narendra Gupta, *Towards Food Secure India,* Indian Science Congress, 2001.

88. *Healthcare Education & IT—The Road Ahead,* National Institute of Science Communication, 2002.

89. Vijayaraghavan, M S, *Information Technology—A Force Multiplier Extraordinary,* DESIDOC Bulletin Info. Technol, 2000.

90. Balakrishnan, N et al., *Emerging Communication Technologies and the Society,* Indian National Science Academy, Narosa Publishing House, 1999.

91. Balakrishnan, A et al., *Novel Substituted Methylenedioxy Lignan Suppresses Proliferation of Cancer Cells by Inhibiting Telomerase and Activation of c-myc and Caspases Leading to Apoptosis,* British J. Cancer, Vol. 87 (1), 2002.

92. Kasturirangan, K, and K R, Sridharamurthy, *ISRO Spacecraft Technology Evolution,* Indian Academy of Sciences, 1998.

93. Tiwari, V M, and R K, Tewari, *The High-Tech War of Twentieth Century,* Vikas Publishing House Pvt. Ltd., 1996.

94. *Proceedings of International Seminar— Force Multiplier Technologies for Naval and Land Warfare,* DRDO, Viva Books Pvt. Ltd., 1999.

95. *Proceedings of the Technical Meet— Navigation & Guidance, Vol. II: Session III,* Astronomical Society of India, 1993.

96. Jensen, Gordon E, and David W, Netzer, *Tactical Missile Propulsion: Vol. 170, Progress in Astronautics and Aeronautics,* AIAA, 1996.

97. Srinivasan, M R, *From Fission to Fusion—The Story of India's Atomic Energy Programme,* Viking Penguin India, 2002.

98. Sullivan, Patrick H, *Value Driven Intellectual Capital,* John Wiley & Sons, 2000.

99. Jalan, Bimal, *India's Economy in the New Millennium,* UBSPD, 2002.

100. Naroola, Gurmeet, *The Entrepreneurial Connection,* Tata McGraw-Hill, 2001.

101. Various Internet Sources & Other Annual Reports.

Index